Sharing Four Cultures

Sharing Four Cultures

A Journey of Love

Barbara Howard Burrus

PROVIDENCE HOUSE PUBLISHERS
Franklin, Tennessee

Printed in the United States of America

00 99 98 97 5 4 3 2 1

Library of Congress Catalog Card Number: 97–66952

ISBN: 1–57736–045–1

Cover by Bozeman Design

Jacket cover photo courtesy of Russell Studio

All author proceeds will go to the Roger-Ellen Foundation to assist the work in health services throughout the world.

PROVIDENCE HOUSE PUBLISHERS
238 Seaboard Lane • Franklin, Tennessee 37067
800-321-5692

I dedicate this book to my soul mate, George, and to our children, Lisa, Laura, Roger, Kate, Ellen, Nan, and Barbara, and to the generations of children to follow. I needed to write this book to share my sixty-four years of life that have been so full of love, joy, and understanding, now to be shared. Here once again in the interior of Africa, I find the opportunity and the incentive to narrate my thoughts. I have done most of my writing in Zaire, Africa, and Snowmass, Colorado, two extremes in climate and scenery. This is a book about four different cultures, their impact on my life, and the opportunity and the privilege George, the family, and I had to be a small part of God's world in the United States, India, Europe, and Africa.

Contents

Sharing Four Cultures

A Journey of Love

Chapter 1

Early Life

I was born July 8, 1931, in Columbia, Tennessee. It was my good fortune to be the firstborn daughter of Louise Judd Howard and Edward Rainey Howard. I was later followed by two sisters, Edwyna, born in 1934, and Gayle, born in 1941.

I am sure that childhood memories, unpleasant as well as pleasant ones, linger throughout one's life. However, looking back, I can remember total love, concern, and well-being given to me through my formative years. My mother says that I was a very serious child, prone to worry, but she saw a very small spark of determination, or stubbornness, which probably served me well in the adventures that lay ahead for me.

My great-grandfather, John Edward Howard Sr., was a grain merchant in Thompson Station, Tennessee, and later the business was called J. E. Howard and Son. The son was my grandfather, Papa Howard. John Edward Howard Sr. was married to Laura Walton, and they were the parents of my grandfather and his two sisters, Aunt Mayne and Aunt Cora. I would like to think that I inherited some of Aunt Mayne's extreme kindness and Aunt Cora's extreme determination. I was privileged to know my great-grandfather and his daughters, Mayne and Cora, but not his wife,

My mother, Louise Judd Howard, and serious Barbara at age two.

Laura, or his son, John, my grandfather. My favorite game as a child was going up the steps to Great-Aunt Cora's house, passing my great-grandfather sitting on the porch with his walking cane and hand outstretched full of pennies. I accepted the pennies, went into the house, out the back door and around the front, up the steps, ready to repeat the game.

John Edward Howard Jr., my grandfather, married Lenora Rainey, and their children were Edward, my father, and Margaret, my aunt, with whom I spent many wonderful days of my early childhood. I called Margaret "Baba," and I was the small flower girl, age four, in her wedding. Her husband was Sam Kinnard, and both Baba and Uncle Sam were very important parts of my life until their deaths in the year 1988. Their son, John Howard Kinnard, was my only first cousin on Daddy's side.

Lenora Rainey Howard, my paternal grandmother, was the best. From the very first, we bonded, understood, and loved each other in an almost spiritual way. Mama Howard, or Miss Nora as my sisters and I called her, was a calm and positive influence on Barbara Jean, her first grandchild.

For some reason, I was closer to my father's family, while my sisters were closer to the Judd side of the family. However, Lillie Mae or Granny Judd, passed her love of flowers and green thumb on to me. She was a lovely lady, talented in gardening and fine stitchery. Her husband, Charles Judd or Granddaddy Judd, was a mixture of fun, teasing, and laughter, and he was very partial to Louise, my mother. He always called her "Baby."

Daddy at Battle Ground Academy.

My father received his early education at Battle Ground Academy in Franklin, Tennessee, traveling by train from Thompson Station, some twenty miles a day. He went to college at the University of Tennessee, changing from a career in medicine to becoming a mortician. He became a partner in Oakes and Nichols Funeral Home in Columbia, Tennessee. He met a pretty blue-eyed girl in Columbia in his early teens, and they married in 1930.

Daddy was a big tease who enjoyed rabbit hunting and running his hounds. His wife, my mother, was talented in organ, piano, and voice. Her voice teacher, Madame Sharp, used to come to the house for lessons, and Edwyna and I would mock them in the next room. Mother was an exceptional homemaker, and our home was full of company and good times. Both of my parents gave my sisters and me love, values to live by, and the security of a healthy self-esteem.

I started school at McDowell Elementary School in Columbia, Tennessee. My first-grade teacher was Miss Junk, and reading and music were my favorite subjects. My stomach would flip when it was time for any kind of artwork. Creativity has never been my strongest

Dressed up for a dance on the drum.

point. My sister Edwyna and I spent countless hours playing with dolls, especially paper dolls. We used Sears and Roebuck catalogs for many of the dolls, furniture, and toys. We pretended by the hours, and even though quite different in nature, we bonded and enjoyed a close relationship that has continued, and I am sure will always exist. Skating, bicycle riding, and snow sledding were other favorite pastimes during my early years, and weekend trips to Daddy's farm to ride our pony, Easter, were big events. My father had Tennessee Walking Horses, and we made the circuit all over Middle Tennessee for the horse shows in the summer. I remember being so pleased when my sister Gayle was born in 1941. Since I was a big ten year old, I felt very responsible for her early buggy rides and later storytelling and baby-sitting. I can remember feeling that I needed to be worthy of her admiration.

Ballet, piano, tap dancing, and violin lessons were parts of my early music appreciation. I never excelled in any of them; however, the exposure was not in vain. I always looked forward to the dance recitals, complete with yards of net, sequins, and satin. Once I wore a satin military uniform and did a tap dance on a large drum. I admit I enjoyed the stage and spotlight. Is it any wonder that my daughter Lisa and her daughter, Jessica, are chips off the old block? I regret that I did not practice the violin after age fourteen, but maybe one of the next generations down the line will use my "fiddle."

When I was twelve, my parents sent me to Camp Monterey for a month of swimming, horseback riding, crafts, hiking, riflery, and tennis. Miss Dolly and Mrs. Sarah Rhodes founded the camp in Monterey, Tennessee, in 1943, and I made friendships there that still exist today. Miss Sarah, at age ninety-five, is a good friend whom I see every Sunday at West End United Methodist Church. However, I am an "inside person" except for gardening and swimming, so camp life was not my favorite thing.

Two individuals who were important in my early years and elementary days in Columbia were Frank Sowell and S. A. Patton. Frank Sowell was a young man my father helped in education and work. He later became the owner of Oakes and Nichols Funeral Home. Years later, George operated on Frank's heart several times. S. A. Patton was a general man of all jobs at Oakes and Nichols. Before my mother and father married, S. A., a black man, roomed with Daddy upstairs over the funeral home. His nickname for me was "Miss Butterball," and his jolly countenance was always a positive influence on me. Sometimes he picked me up from school, and one Easter Sunday morning sticks in my memory very vividly. When I was five, he willingly carried me into Sunday school to protect my new patent shoes from the deep snow. He enjoyed helping with Mr. Ed's girls.

My freshman year at Columbia High School was especially enjoyable due to my clarinet playing in the school band. I marched and marched with my blue and gold band uniform, shiny black clarinet, and feather in my cap. Once the bass drum player made a wrong turn, and being so involved in my music, I followed him down the field, opposite from the rest of the band.

High school proms and frills.

My family moved to Franklin, Tennessee, in 1945. For some reason, Franklin seemed more like home to me than Columbia until I married in 1953. I enjoyed my sophomore year at Franklin High School, being a part of the homecoming court at Franklin High, and dances and sporting events at Battle Ground Academy.

However, the highlight of these years was my involvement in my youth group at Franklin United Methodist Church. I will always treasure the friendships, values, and self-esteem that resulted from my participation in the United Methodist Youth Fellowship program. I met my lifelong best friend, Catherine Hardison, along with other good buddies, Connie Ewin, Marie Hardison, John Beasley, Daly Thompson, and Tommy Butts. After every Sunday evening's program, we adjourned to someone's house where a piano was available, and we spent hours singing and continuing the evening's fellowship. Usually, John played while Catherine and Connie sang for the group. That summer of 1945, I

The old hotel at Beersheba Springs where I met George.

attended my first youth camp at Beersheba Springs, Tennessee. The Tennessee Conference of the United Methodist Church owned some land at Beersheba, and the old hotel, once the scene of society gatherings, was used for camping and meeting experiences of Middle Tennessee United Methodists for all ages.

In many ways, my story and adventure begins at this point, because at age fifteen, I met George Robert Burrus at Beersheba Springs Youth Camp. My girlfriends and I were in the lobby of the old hotel watching some boys play Ping-Pong. I noticed the enthusiastic blond boy jumping around the table, and as he passed the first time, he asked, "What's your name?" The second time around he said, "I'm George Burrus." Needless to say, he captured my attention. Sometimes we were square-dance partners, shared a hymnal during vespers, or just happened to eat at the same table.

Two special adult friends of the period at Beersheba were Dr. Jack Walton and Jane Hamblin Batts. They both entered my life in later years once again, as "Dr. Jack" officiated at my daughter Lisa's wedding, and Jane was quoted in an article about Beersheba days.

> A story Jane tells illustrates her belief in the church as a fellowship. When Lloyd Loftis, a member of First Church, Cookeville, was about to undergo heart by-pass surgery last year, Jane visited him in the hospital. He produced a sketch his surgeon, Dr. Burrus, had drawn to show the procedure that would be carried out the next day. Jane asked if the surgeon's first name was George. If it was, she told him, then he and his doctor had something in common—a fondness for recalling their camp experiences at Beersheba Springs Assembly. She added: "If it turns out to be Dr. George Burrus, I'll feel all the better about you!" And sure enough, it was. Loftis later told how the night before his surgery, he and the surgeon got to know each other better through sharing the meaning Beersheba had for each of them. "This," said Jane, "is an example of Christian fellowship—warm, dynamic, creative. And it's everywhere!"

George became the president of the Tennessee Conference Youth Fellowship, and my job was secretary. These offices entitled us to summer trips to Lake Junaluska, North Carolina, for youth camps. The fellowship with other officers was a big plus for our relationship, and through the years, we have been back many times for vacations and visits to friends living there. Our favorite fall weekend trip is to see Bess and Ben St. Clair, longtime friends. Ben was our pastor at West End United Methodist Church, but more about Ben and Bess later. In 1947, George and I were part of a group of ten thousand young people headed for Cleveland, Ohio, and the Cleveland Conference. We rode the train from Nashville to Cleveland and renewed our summer friendship. We both had other friends on board, but still gave each other the "eye."

The next fall I entered Peabody Demonstration School in Nashville for my junior year of high school. It was my third and last high school,

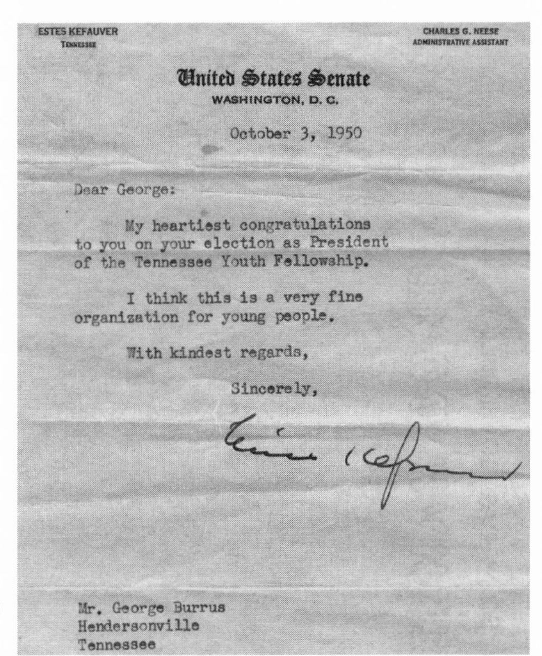
ESTES KEFAUVER
TENNESSEE

CHARLES G. NEESE
ADMINISTRATIVE ASSISTANT

United States Senate
WASHINGTON, D. C.

October 3, 1950

Dear George:

My heartiest congratulations to you on your election as President of the Tennessee Youth Fellowship.

I think this is a very fine organization for young people.

With kindest regards,

Sincerely,

Mr. George Burrus
Hendersonville
Tennessee

A letter from Senator Estes Kefauver to George.

and I graduated from Peabody in 1949. Each high school was a pleasant experience and gave me the opportunity years later of having friends in Columbia, Franklin, and Nashville.

Three of my future sisters-in-law became good friends during my high school years. Even before we knew about the Burrus Boys, Emily Abernathy, Marianne Calhoun, and Mary Joyce Niederhauser were my friends at Beersheba Church Camp and Peabody Demonstration School. The four of us have remained close friends through the years and shared family sadness and joys, as well as young years as mothers and more mature years as grandmothers. Another special friend of this period was Evalina Casey. I spent many wonderful weekends at her family home in Franklin for Battle Ground Academy dances. Usually, a group of Nashville and Franklin girls spent the weekend, and we talked and talked until dawn. Catherine Hardison Brent, Evalina Casey Cheadle, and I still meet for lunch often, some forty years later. Strong friendships are a special part of one's mature years.

My senior prom at Peabody Demonstration School. My date, George, and best friend, Catherine Hardison Brent.

During my final geometry exam as a junior in 1948, I just happened to glance at the upper glass door in the classroom. There stood George Burrus peering in, and just as quickly disappearing. Geometry was never my best subject, so I turned in my paper and strolled to the front steps of Peabody Demonstration School, and there stood George. If they ever tear down the school, I want a piece of the steps, because there George asked me for our first date. The date was for his senior picnic at Cedars of Lebanon, a swimming complex and picnic grounds. George was graduating from Duncan School, a small school for boys near the Vanderbilt campus, and would enter Vanderbilt premed the following fall.

After graduation from Peabody Demonstration School in 1949, I entered Martin Methodist College in Pulaski, Tennessee, some eighty-five miles south of Franklin. Martin College was a junior college founded in 1870, and in 1993, it became a four-year institution.

The first year at Martin College I roomed with Peggy Jo Thompson from Sango, Tennessee. She was a sophomore student, and a very charming and sincere Christian girl. I always felt that year was special since she was my friend in thought, word, and deed. There was no one as down to earth as Peggy Jo. I was a bridesmaid in her wedding years later, but I lost contact with her during the early sixties.

My roommate during my second year at Martin College was Betty B. Garrett from Nashville. Betty B. and I bonded, and our friendship has continued through the years. She was one of six children in a family that was a role model for me in later years. Mrs. Garrett was full of so much compassion that her inner self was revealed in words and deeds of magnitude. She always displayed many pictures of her family, and maybe that was my inspiration for the same deed in later years. My weekends at their home were full of fun times, and they just happened to live near George Burrus's home in Hendersonville.

The summer after I graduated from Martin College I took a summer job at Beersheba Springs Campgrounds. My job description was part-time office worker and part-time worker in the dining room. The entire summer was a learning experience in many ways. Local mountain girls worked with me in the dining room, and this was my first of many experiences dealing with people from other backgrounds and the challenge of understanding other cultural experiences. They soon realized that I was shocked by their street-wise conversations. However, by the end of summer, we had reached a common ground of give-and-take and somewhat of a better relationship.

That fall I entered Peabody College in Nashville. I was a day student and rode the Franklin Interurban Bus each day from Franklin to Nashville. I was anxious to help out on my tuition during my last two years of college, so I worked part-time in the office at Franklin United Methodist Church. My major at Peabody was elementary education, and I prepared to teach the primary grades, a wise choice for later years when I taught my own children in other countries. Three good friends in college were Joan Pelot from Crossville, Tennessee, Ann Harris from Nashville, and Eunice Batey from Birmingham, Alabama. All three friends remained a part of my adult years. Eunice married Harry Goodall, an undergraduate classmate of George at Vanderbilt, and later as Dr. and Mrs. Harry Goodall, they went to Africa as medical missionaries. Eunice was killed in a small plane crash in the 1960s. It was our good fortune to know her children and grandchildren in Africa. However, I am getting eighteen or so years ahead of my tale. Ann Harris married a med-school friend of George's, Phillip Porch, and George and I were in their wedding in 1952. Ann's path and mine have crossed at weddings, funerals, and parties over the years. It is always a treat to meet up with Ann. Joan Pelot, another elementary education major, married Jack Rice, a member of George's medical class. Jack's brother, Hal, married George's first cousin, Martha Swan Shaw, so naturally our paths crossed through the years. During my Peabody College days, I often met George for lunch at the Vanderbilt Hospital cafeteria. We usually dated on the weekends. His studies came first though, and that was my early training for being the wife of a doctor.

As an elementary education major, I enjoyed one semester of practice teaching at Peabody Demonstration School in the first grade, and one semester at a Nashville city school called Eakin Elementary School. The principal at Eakin was Mrs. Ina Trimble, and even though I was a student teacher, we began a friendship that lasted many years.

George invited me to spend a weekend with his family in Hendersonville in early April 1953, and I left school that Friday afternoon telling my friends that I would return on Monday with a ring. I knew he had purchased one because my parents owned Franklin Jewelers and he had already picked up the ring. Friday night passed and no ring! All day Saturday passed and no ring! I dreaded going to classes on Monday. On Sunday afternoon, George had to check out the tobacco field for his father, and we rode the same horse out to the field. I was sitting in front, and as we gazed at the scenery, he reached around me with the ring!

George's father was a general practitioner in Nashville for thirty years. George had three brothers, Bill, Roger, and Swan, and two sisters, Catherine Dale and Laurale.

I always said that getting my college degree came before getting married. So I graduated from Peabody College on Friday night, June 5, 1953, and married on Monday afternoon, June 8, 1953. Our wedding took place at Franklin United Methodist Church at four-thirty on a hot

Cutting the cake—June 8, 1953.

and humid afternoon. It was the summer between George's sophomore and junior years in medical school. After our wedding, we left for a honeymoon in Washington, D.C., and New York City. We enjoyed the usual visitors' sights, but decided to head back to Beersheba Springs for a few days of quiet mountain simplicity.

After George and I returned from our honeymoon, we settled into a small two-bedroom house on the Burrus farm, Maple Row, in Hendersonville, Tennessee. It was a comfortable rock and stucco house, and we felt fortunate that Dr. and Mrs. Burrus provided it for us. I enjoyed unpacking lovely wedding gifts and making a nest for George and me. I had no idea how many "nests" lay ahead for me to create. George was beginning his junior year in medical school that summer, and I worked as a secretary for the Geography Department at Peabody College. During the spring before our marriage, I had secured a job with the Nashville City Schools as a second-grade teacher at Eakin

Elementary School. Mrs. Trimble had asked for me as a teacher, and it was a blessing to have her guidance as friend and principal.

Our first car that fall of 1953 was a pale blue Plymouth. We left Hendersonville each morning by six o'clock in order to drive the eighteen miles into Nashville for my teaching job and his Vanderbilt Medical School classes. George drove me to Eakin, then took the car on to Vanderbilt because he would not come home until ten or eleven that evening. After school, I took the city bus to downtown Nashville and changed to another bus, which carried me to Gallatin Road in East Nashville. George's father, Dr. Roger Burrus, had a clinic at 3917 Gallatin Road, and I waited there to ride to Hendersonville with Dr. Burrus after his office hours. We usually arrived at the Burrus home around five or six o'clock, and most nights, I ate with Doctor, Mama B., and Aunt Mary, sister of Mrs. Burrus and nurse for Dr. Burrus. After dinner, I prepared for the next day's schoolwork and went to bed. Around eleven o'clock, George tapped me on the shoulder to go to our house. The next morning we got up early and repeated our routine. Someone might ask why I did not go to my own house each evening. The truth was that I was afraid to be alone in our little guest house far from neighbors.

My first year of teaching was full of new and rewarding experiences with my class of thirty second graders. Somehow, I chose the right profession for my personality, and it would also serve me well teaching my own children in later years.

My relationship with some of my fellow teachers has lasted long after my teaching for four years at Eakin School. Two teachers stand out as an example—Virginia Beasley, a Peabody classmate, taught the third grade, as did Ellen White Dillon. Virginia was company for me while George worked late on weekends, and her family opened their home to me on many occasions. Ellen and I were good friends, but if we could have caught a glimpse of the future, we would have seen our daughters as best friends, my daughter Laura wearing Ellen's wedding dress, and our grandchildren as playmates. Another favorite fellow teacher was Elinor Ewing, a lady in every sense of the word. Years later, we would enjoy meeting at the Centennial Club, a mutual club for social and educational programs.

After my first year of teaching and George's junior year in medical school, we looked forward to a summer of rest and less routine. Each morning George and I arose early and swam across the Cumberland River. George carried an inner tube strapped to his ankle in case I felt tired, and we enjoyed the challenge. However, when Dr. Burrus found out about this activity, he squelched the idea for safety reasons.

Also, that summer of 1954 was an opportunity for George to earn some extra money by working each evening in the laboratory at Nashville General Hospital. On his last night of work in the laboratory, I had gone to a Billy Graham Crusade in Nashville with my friend, Virginia Beasley. After I took Virginia home and was on my way to pick up George, I unfortunately ran a stop sign in front of Eakin School. A car hit me on the passenger side, knocking me into the stop sign across the street, and consequently, a new door had to be purchased for the car. We had to use all of the money that George earned that summer to buy a new door for the car. Another by-product of the accident was that the next morning when I arrived at Eakin School, my students were so excited as they exclaimed, "Mrs. Burrus, Mrs. Burrus, did you hear about the dumb lady that hit the stop sign in front of school last night?" "No," I said, "tell me about the dumb lady that hit the stop sign." Fortunately, the driver of the other car, a school parent, had withheld my name! School began with a bang that year!

It became increasingly difficult for George and me to make the twenty-mile trip each day from Hendersonville into Nashville for teaching and medical school. We began to apartment hunt and found a small one-bedroom apartment in a private home very close to Eakin School and Vanderbilt University. We were reluctant to leave our first little guest house, but the move made it possible for me to keep the car, come home after school, and go over to Vanderbilt to have dinner with George each evening. The move also gave me the opportunity to tutor students in the summer months since we lived in their community close to Eakin School.

George graduated from Vanderbilt University in the spring of 1955. I can remember his father's proud words to me as George received his Doctor of Medicine degree. He turned to me and said, "That's our boy!" Indeed, he was "our boy," and he has never used his degree in any way other than service to his fellow human beings. That was the first of many times to follow that I experienced pride and joy in George's accomplishments.

The next step was a year of surgical internship at Vanderbilt Hospital. Eight young doctors made up the class and brought eight young wives together to forge friendships lasting for many years; Lucy and Arnold Killen, Kathleen and Terry Rees, Elizabeth and Gene Regen, Melba and Bob Youngblood, Jackie and Jim Guest, Cynthia and Jim Pitcock, and Teri and Jack Lyons entered our life to enrich it throughout the years.

George began his first year of general surgical residency at Vanderbilt in July of 1956. We had moved to the residency apartments at the Veterans Hospital on White Bridge Road and enjoyed the company of other young residents living so close. These buildings have been replaced by Nashville School of Technology. We were anxious to start our family, and on February 24, 1957, our firstborn gave us joy and thanksgiving for her birth. We named her Lisa, and for us, it was the beginning of the most rewarding of all journeys, that of being parents.

After finishing his first year of residency at Vanderbilt, George decided to ask Dr. William Scott to help him secure his cardiothoracic training in Houston, Texas, with two of the pioneers in heart surgery, Dr. Michael DeBakey and Dr. Denton Cooley. We had been in touch with the Methodist Board of Missions in New York from time to time about our future as missionaries in a foreign country. However, they were concerned about George getting too much sophisticated training for the mission field, but he wanted the best, and he felt that our four years in Houston would give him the opportunity to receive the best available cardiac surgery residency.

In July of 1957, we packed up our entire belongings on a trailer attached to our Plymouth, gathered up our Lisa, and headed for Houston and the unknown. A few weeks before we left I had called my father and said that the worst thing was going to happen! I told him that we were leaving for Houston, Texas. Since it was my first journey west of the Mississippi, it was like going to a foreign land. Little did I know how far my journey would take me in later years. On the way to Houston, we ran into Hurricane Audrey in Louisiana and had some rain damage to our personal belongings. But being young and adventurous, we took it in stride and rode down South Main Street in Houston ready to meet what would lie ahead.

Our first order of business was to find an apartment close to the Medical Center, and after a lengthy search, we found one on Bolsover Road, a dead-end street with old, comfortable houses. We rented the downstairs of a private home, and the owners, three sisters, lived upstairs. One sister was in real estate and did not mean to rent to a family with children. However, she was out of town, and another sister said, "Move on in!" We lived there for three years, had two more children, and enjoyed a good relationship with the Wharton sisters.

During our three years on Bolsover Road, we were blessed with the addition of Laura, born in 1958, and George Roger, born in 1960. Laura was the name of my paternal great-grandmother, and Roger was named after his grandfather and father. Many professors of Rice University lived on our street; therefore, Lisa, Laura, and Roger had plenty of playmates.

Our money was very limited, and George worked long and hard hours, but we always think of our days in Houston, Texas, as very good and productive years. During one three-month rotation with Dr. DeBakey, George came home only three times. One of the times Dr. DeBakey was in Russia, so George felt safe to come home for a few hours.

A favorite outing with the children was a trip to Hermann Park to see the zoo and ride the small train that runs throughout the park. How interesting it is that thirty-six years later, one of my grandchildren, Katie Cox, would visit Hermann Park with her Houston grandmother, Ann Cox, and ride the same train as Lisa, Laura, and Roger had done in 1960.

In the fall of 1959, I received the unexpected news of my father's death by heart attack in Franklin, Tennessee. Edwyna was living in Corpus Christi, Texas, at the time, and she joined the children, George, and me for our trip back home. "Big Daddy," as Lisa called him, was only fifty years old, and I shall always remember his mother's tears for her only son. Already I missed my father's easy disposition and pleasing nature. How he would have loved to see and play with his great-grand-children!

After three years in the apartment on Bolsover Road, we moved to a small house with a fenced-in backyard. George's older brother Swan and his family moved to Houston for additional training at M. D. Anderson Cancer Center and were close neighbors. The year was 1961, and again, we were blessed with another daughter, Kate.

For me, four children under the age of four years was a welcomed challenge. I had no help, but each day I spent doing what I liked best, being a mother. The former British prime minister, Mrs. Margaret Thatcher, said it best for me in her biography: "The pull of a mother towards her children is perhaps the strongest and most instinctive emotion we have. I was never one of those people who regarded being 'just' a mother or 'just' a housewife as second best. To be a mother and a housewife is a vocation of a very high kind."

On the day that our Kate was born in March 1961, George was on Dr. Denton Cooley's service at Texas Children's Hospital. George asked for permission to go over to Methodist Hospital for Kate's birth, and when he returned, Dr. Cooley, the father of five daughters, asked about the baby. As a joke, George replied that he had a baby boy. No comment came from Dr. Cooley's side of the operating table. Later on in the evening during hospital rounds, George told Dr. Cooley that he "could not tell a lie, the baby was a girl." At that time, Dr. Cooley playfully slapped him on the back, saying, "I knew you were not man enough to have another boy."

George finished his thoracic surgery residency in 1961, and we left Houston to go back to Nashville. George's father, Dr. Roger Burrus, or "Grand" as the grandchildren called him, had become ill with cancer of the bladder. He and Mrs. Burrus, known as "Poppi," flew to M. D. Anderson Hospital in Houston for treatment, as we went home to carry on his practice. We lived in Hendersonville once again, and Lisa attended Miss Nanny's kindergarten.

CHAPTER 2

Adventure Begins
India, 1962–1963

For many years, George had the dream of going to another land to be a doctor. We had been in touch with the Methodist Board of Missions for several years. After his excellent training with Dr. DeBakey and Dr. Cooley, we spent one year in Nashville helping with Grand's practice after his death in 1961. However, we went ahead with our contact with the Board, and after several courses at Scarritt College and many preparations, we were ready to go to Nadiad, India, for five years of medical mission work.

I can remember Grandmother Howard's disbelief as we packed up our belongings to be shipped to a faraway place for five years. The shipment included my wedding china, crystal, and a three-by-three-foot gold leaf mirror given to me by my bridesmaids. After all, I planned to make a home in India for my family. Because I was still a young age of thirty-one years, it was with a feeling of anticipation of great adventure into the unknown, plus it would not have mattered where I went as long as I was with George!

In July of 1962, we crossed the Atlantic on the *Queen Elizabeth I*. We left the harbor in New York City bound for an adventure in a land of different culture, sights, and sounds. How young and naive I was!

Anne Hathaway's cottage, England.

Our family at that point consisted of George (age 31), Barbara (age 31), Lisa (age 5), Laura (age 3), Roger (age 2), Kate (age 1), and a baby yet to be born. Our accommodations on the *Queen Elizabeth I* were less than first class. We could not open our porthole because we were below the water line. We had two small rooms separated by another person's cabin. Each room accommodated three or four persons with bunk beds. I stayed in one room with two children, and George stayed with two.

I felt very seasick from the beginning and took to my bunk bed, while George and the children viewed the Statue of Liberty as we sailed away from America. I need to digress for a few lines to say that thirty-one years later, we crossed the Atlantic on the *Queen Elizabeth II* for our fortieth wedding anniversary. George and I shared a large stateroom with dressing room and bath; we enjoyed first-class dining, no seasickness, and the captain's reception. We also watched the Statue of Liberty, welcoming us home to children and, by that time, grandchildren! But back to my journey to India. Lisa enjoyed the nursery on the *Queen Elizabeth I* where, unbeknownst to us, she was exposed to chicken pox.

We landed in Southampton, England, and were due to leave for Bombay, India, two weeks later from the port of Liverpool, England. It was very exciting to be in London, England, for two whole weeks. We were very comfortable in a small hotel with one large room and two baby beds. Every day, we set out to see the sights—Tower of London, Buckingham Palace, Westminster Abbey, Big Ben, Windsor Castle, and several tours around the city, always trying to keep the four children

Blenheim Palace.

reasonably quiet and in tow! However, after three or four days of that routine, we decided to rent a car and make our way to Liverpool.

We left the hotel and piled into a small English car. After receiving directions, we set out for the countryside. One hour later, we came to a town much the size of London. I rolled down the window and asked where we were. The bobby said, "London, ma'am." We had come back within a block of the small hotel that we had left one hour ago. So much for English directions!

Safely on our way again, we headed toward Shakespeare country, Stratford-upon-Avon, and to the small thatched-roof cottage of Anne Hathaway. George gave me the opportunity to quickly go through the cottage while he circled the block with the four children in the car. The only impression I remembered was the bench where Anne and William Shakespeare courted. Years later, I slowly made the tour again, without rushing in and out of the cottage.

Each night we stopped at a small inn. We ate dinner and breakfast there, then had the innkeeper pack us a lunch for the noon picnic that day somewhere out in the countryside. We stopped along the way to picnic, watch a cricket game, or visit somewhere important, such as Blenheim Palace, the birthplace of Sir Winston Churchill. Thirty-three years later, I would dine in the palace, but more about that later.

We made our journey north through Wales to Blackpool, a seaside resort, and on to our ultimate goal, which was Liverpool, the site of our departure for Bombay. The following letter was written to my mother after we arrived in England:

Sunday
July 15, 1962

Dearest Mimi,

Well, our first boat trip is over, and we were so glad to see land again! I was seasick for two days, but none of the bunch were sick at all. After the *Queen Elizabeth* docked 1st in France, we went on to England where we got off the boat. Going through customs wasn't too bad, then we boarded a train for London. After two hours' ride we finally arrived at the famous Waterloo Station, then on to our hotel. Clean beds and a large room were a welcome sight by then! We stayed in London three days and saw Buckingham Palace, Tower of London (an old castle), Westminster Abbey, other royal palaces etc. and saw two excellent stage musicals, *My Fair Lady* and *Sound of Music*. After having seen *My Fair Lady* twice in two weeks I would suggest anyone saving up and going to New York just to see it!!

Our boat for Bombay leaves Liverpool on the 21st of July so we rented a small English car and are driving for a week over England! We visited Oxford yesterday and stopped last night at a small English village inn. Well the food was the first American tasting food that we have had since leaving New York, so we decided to stay over until in the morning. We went to the village church today. This time is 7 hr. ahead of Tennessee so we finish supper before your lunch!

Tomorrow we are going up to Stratford-upon-Avon, Shakespeare country, and view his home and etc. George is holding out fairly well putting up with domestic duties! I wish you could see him driving this English car with the steering wheel on the right and driving on the left side of the road. The girls and Roger are fine and not missing a trick!

I'll write again as soon as we get settled on the boat. It is taking us 6 wk. in all to get there and I'm sure we will all be glad to get settled! Nothing like a journey of this sort to tax a mama's sense of humor! Ha! Pass this letter on to Gayle and Edwyna. I've written them, but not in this detail! I am anxious for news of home so let me hear at the India address. Take care of yourself and we all love you.

Barbara, George, Lisa, Laura, Roger, Kate

Upon arriving in Liverpool, we found our ship, the *Circassius*, in port and already boarding the crew and people for Bombay. We had lots of dirty clothes, and our expectations for living accommodations were not met, being very meager, plus sharing a bath with other passengers. I guess you might say that I became unglued, so George changed our room for an upper deck room and private bath. It had a porthole for the passing scenery. Both the private bath and the porthole proved blessings, as I relate the long, hot, and tedious journey.

We left Liverpool in mid-July and headed for the Strait of Gibraltar and the beautiful Mediterranean. The children enjoyed the sights and sounds of the boat, and the trip was fairly smooth until the chicken pox struck! And strike it did! All four children, Lisa, Laura, Roger, and Kate, were quarantined for two weeks in our room. The steward brought their meals to the room and watched the children while George and I went to the dining room. Kate was the only one, at age one year, we kept in the baby bed for safety reasons. She paced that baby bed like a baby lion for two weeks. A Scottish doctor on board came in every day to count heads and make sure that we were keeping the children quarantined. One day, as he counted three children and seemed upset, Lisa popped out from the upper bunk and startled him. We all had a good laugh after he left.

As our boat left the smooth Mediterranean Sea, we entered the Suez Canal and encountered very hot weather. The children enjoyed looking out of the porthole and seeing the desert scenes on shore, especially the camels. Once out of the canal, we entered the Red Sea, then on to the Indian Ocean and the port of Karachi, Pakistan.

During the trip, I had made friends with a young Pakistani mother of three children. Often, we sat on deck with a cup of tea and exchanged stories of motherhood. She and her husband were returning to Pakistan after five years in England. Since we were on our way to India for five years, I was interested in her homecoming. I asked her who would be meeting them in Karachi, and she replied that her husband's first wife would meet them. She explained her situation. She was a Muslim, and since her husband's wife could not give him children, he had taken a second wife. Upon their return, she explained, they would all live together. I asked about the duties of the household, such as cleaning and cooking, and she said that they would share everything, even the husband, I guess!

I went back to the cabin and told George that I had to be up on deck the next morning to see wife number one greet wife number two, the husband, and children. The next morning I witnessed much embracing and many presents for the children, and the last I saw of them was a picture of family harmony going down the road. She had told me that life was not meant to be full of strife and selfishness, but she was a better woman than I!

When we landed in Bombay, the authorities quickly let us and our children, with many pox marks, get off the boat first because they were afraid of smallpox. We spent a few nights in Bombay, then boarded a train, called the Gujarat Mail, bound for Nadiad, India, 250 miles north of Bombay. Gujarat was the name of the state, and Nadiad was our rural village. The train was full, inside and out, with the overflow of people riding on top of the train. We spent the night on the train and stopped at every village. I can remember looking out of the window at each stop and seeing people sleeping everywhere on the sidewalk between the train and station.

My very first impression was one of a tropical and steamy atmosphere, filled with the sounds and smells of a new and very different culture.

We were met in Nadiad by Ola and Jim McClendon and their two small sons, Mark and Matthew. We lived with them for a few weeks, during which time George had typhoid fever. I gave baths to all four children three or four times a day to guard against infection from their pox marks.

We soon were all well again and moved into a two-story home that was the initial site of the clinic and home of Dr. and Mrs. Corporon who initiated the medical work in Nadiad in 1908. The garden included a small tennis court and a lovely teahouse. Over the years the house was enlarged, and consequently, we had plenty of space for family activities. Upstairs we had a large recreation room that was used for tricycles and ball games.

We settled in, hung the gold leaf mirror, and became acquainted with our cook, Cordabhi, our ayah (nurse), Ruthbhi, and our sweeper, Marium. One of the first items of the household was to do away with a fancy tea at four or four-thirty in the afternoon. The children loved the British custom with fancy cakes and sandwiches, but it spoiled dinner for them. Also, George did not see the need for the break before he was finished for the day at the hospital.

Each morning, Cordabhi and I sat down and went over the food for the day, then he jumped on his bicycle and headed for the bazaar or market. He understood some of my English, but his language was Gujarati, a dialect of Hindi. We kept household accounts, so I caught on to the money value, kitchen vocabulary, and how to run a household in a vastly different culture. His caste was that of a cook, and one day he explained to us through an interpreter that he was being disgraced by taking out the garbage. He insisted that it was Marium's job. After much discussion and slight panic on my side, we compromised, and George said that he would carry it out at night if Cordabhi would carry it out in the morning. That suited the cook, so a crisis was avoided.

The children's favorite pastime was running to the front gate at the sound of a twinkling bell. The bell meant that an elephant was passing in front of our house. The elephant carried a sign on his back that advertised

My four bunnies in India—Lisa, Laura, Roger, and Kate.

the local movie in town. Another treat for the children was a dancing bear that came by often to perform. His owner always expected a tip.

Nadiad was a small town between Baroda and Ahmadabad, the fifth largest city in India. Often, we went to Ahmadabad for a shopping trip or a visit to the wonderful zoo. The city was full of people, cows, and three-wheeled taxis. A ride in one of the vehicles was not soon to be forgotten. Sometimes we rode the train to Ahmadabad or took our hospital car. Once, we stopped by the roadside and let Lisa ride an elephant. I wonder if she remembers this "big deal." The stores in the teeming city were full of beautiful silks, brass, and other Indian treasures, only to be viewed and not to be purchased on a missionary's salary.

My mornings were busy with school lessons for Lisa's first-grade work. The old house was so large that we easily had a big schoolroom for this purpose. We used the Calvert System, located in Baltimore, Maryland, and the company sent every book or material needed for grades one through twelve. George had the carpenters at the hospital build a large sandbox on legs for our use in social studies, and we even used a colorful Indian abacus found in the bazaar in Nadiad. Laura, Roger, and Kate played in the large room upstairs with Marium while school was in progress.

One of my favorite India stories is about a dinner that we attended at a textile mill owner's home in Ahmadabad. Since it was a dinner with meat, his wife would not enter the dining room, so I was the only female present. His son was a professional dancer of Indian interpretations, and after dinner, we removed our shoes and filed into a room with soft lighting and giant pillows in a circle on the floor. Somehow, George ended up on a pillow across the room, and as the dance progressed, I noticed that he was sound asleep, plus he had a big hole in one of his socks. I tried in vain to get someone's attention, hoping that our host would not notice the sleeping doctor.

The following letter written by George to send home our first Christmas gives some of the details of the trip to India and the situation there in the hospital:

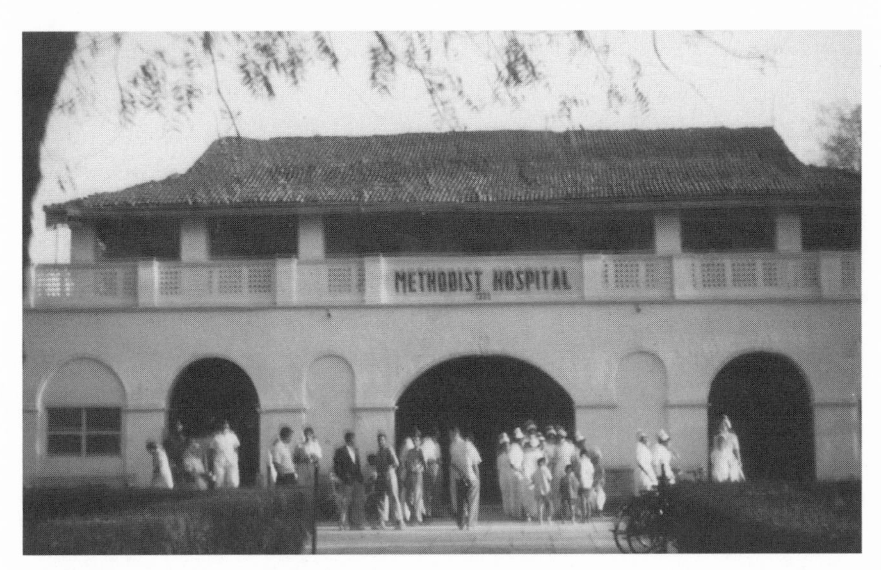

Methodist Hospital—Nadiad, India.

Methodist Hospital
Nadiad, India
January 11, 1963

Dear Friends,

We have tried to answer all of our mail as promptly as possible, but we realize that there are many persons whom we promised to write. We hope this general informational letter will serve the purpose of bringing you up to date with our family and our first six months here in Nadiad.

Mother Howard and the families put us on board the plane in Nashville on July the second, and Mother Burrus saw us aboard the *Queen Elizabeth* July the fifth. The trip to India was very interesting. Our first stop was London, where we saw the sights, including the "Changing of the Guard" at Buckingham Palace, Westminster Abbey, and Aldersgate Street.

From there we made our way to Liverpool, stopping at Blenheim Castle, the birthplace of Sir Winston Churchill, Stratford-upon-Avon, and Oxford. The English countryside was very well kept from this farm boy's viewpoint. The roads were well paved, but very narrow and crooked. Once we learned to stay on the wrong side of the road, the trip in our little Ford was most delightful.

We left Liverpool by boat on July the twenty-first, and the thing that worried George the most was that we were only going sixteen miles an hour! The Rock of Gibraltar was as impressive as the Prudential sign would lead you to believe. In the middle of the Mediterranean Sea the children started having the chickenpox and were confined to the cabin. From then on we really began to look forward to landing in Bombay. After going through the Suez Canal and passing through the area where Moses crossed the Red Sea we realized that he was not only a great law giver, but also a great optimist to believe that there was a land flowing with milk and honey the other side of that hot and barren desert. However, the children enjoyed seeing the camels from our porthole, and didn't seem to mind the intense heat of the desert.

Dr. and Mrs. Aldrich were waiting on the dock to greet us in Bombay. We managed to get our medical equipment through customs without too much difficulty, and took the overnight train from Bombay to Nadiad. Nadiad is about 250 miles north of Bombay, and the hospital was first established here in 1908, and has a bed capacity of 150. George went right to work at the hospital as Dr. Aldrich had many matters to clear up before leaving Nadiad. We stayed with Dr. and Mrs. Jim McClendon for about four weeks, and moved into our house the middle of September.

George is running the surgical service which includes the surgical specialties, obstetrics, and gynecology. Jim McClendon runs the medical service which includes diagnostic radiology and pediatrics. There are two residents and usually two or three interns. Miss Lorenz is the head of the nursing service and also runs our nursing school. She is justly proud of the fact that one of her recent graduates was the top student in our state of Gujarat. Miss Gallagher is the head of the laboratory and along with her technicians adds greatly to the care of our patients.

We operate six days a week, and sometimes on Sunday, and see patients in the clinics five afternoons a week. Our operative cases range from tooth extraction to esophagectomy, and we are able to do our chest surgery only because of the generous gifts of the thoracic instruments.

There are very few people in this area doing Thoracic Surgery while there are many cases of tuberculosis, bronchiectasis, tumor, and heart disease. We see many far advanced and often times neglected cases of infection and tumor. We also see such diseases as leprosy, elephantiasis, fluke infection, and echinococcus cysts. Hookworm and tuberculosis are rampant, and malnutrition is a partner in many of our cases. We are lucky when the hemoglobins on our patients are above 10 grams, and many of our obstetrical cases come in and deliver with a hemoglobin below 5 grams.

We have fixed up a schoolroom within our house where Lisa, our six year old is studying her first grade work by the Calvert School method. This Calvert School material is used world-wide, and a portion of each morning is set aside for reading, numbers, art activities, science, stories, and sounds. Laura, our four year old, joins in for many of the activities everyday. Roger, who is three years, and Kate, our two year old, enjoy a large upstairs playroom while school is in progress.

We are studying the language four times a week, and find it very difficult to read and write. The alphabet of the Gujarati language is entirely new for us, however we can see why it is important to be able to communicate with the people in work, recreation, and worship.

We hope to be hearing from many of you, and may the New Year of 1963 be one of Peace for all.

Your missionaries,

Barbara and George Burrus

George tells the story that he once visited a local judge on the matter of job clarification at the hospital. The Indian workers felt that a job was a job for life, no matter how well or poorly that you performed. The judge had his servants bring in two tall, cool glasses of what looked like milk shakes. He said it was a "special" Indian treat of soured milk. George took a big gulp and nearly choked. The judge was amused and offered him a Coke; George quickly took the offer.

George once operated on a guru, or holy man, of the Hindu religion. He was the guru of Mr. Mafatlal, owner of New Shoroc Mills, a large cotton mill in Nadiad. Some said that Mr. Mafatlal was the John D. Rockefeller of India. Dr. McClendon asked George to see the guru for prostate trouble. He also had bad lungs and heart, and he smoked many "bidis," small Indian cigarettes, every day. George said it was risky to operate, but he put a supra pubic tube in the bladder. The procedure went well, but he received word to come by the guru's room.

The guru told George that he had made a monkey out of him by giving him a tail, referring to the tube in his bladder. They talked further about the risk of a prostatectomy. However, the guru said to go ahead with the surgery. He would pick an auspicious day for the surgery and everything would be fine! Dr. McClendon agreed to the surgery, and the guru tolerated the procedure quite well.

George and son, Roger, playing cricket in India.

Mr. Mafatlal installed an air conditioner in the room for further patients, and I was a benefactor of the convenience when Ellen was born. Weeks later, I sent word to George at the hospital that Mr. Mafatlal was at our home. He rushed home on his bicycle, and Mr. Mafatlal again thanked him and gave him 100,000 rupees (about $15,000) for the hospital work.

I had some tooth problems in India and inquired about a dentist. A Chinese dentist was recommended to me, and I made an appointment. His methods were not very up-to-date, and it was a new experience for me to see the dentist use a drill operated by foot while working on my mouth. Before beginning the work, he had swabbed out my mouth with some sort of liquid. When he left the room, I took a peek at the liquid used and found that it was Dettal, the same detergent that I used on my floors at home. We became friends with the dentist and his wife, and George delivered a fine son for them sometime later.

George had several interns from local medical schools in Baroda and Ahmadabad and residents from Vellore Medical School in Mysore State to come to Nadiad to work with him and Jim McClendon. Among these interns was Suresh Ramnath, who was particularly effective and spent some extra time at the hospital. After his training in India,

Common transportation in India.

Suresh went to Canada for further medical work, then he contacted George in Nashville. George helped him obtain a neurosurgery residency with Dr. William Meacham at Vanderbilt, who most graciously accepted George's recommendation. During his residency, Suresh was a frequent visitor in our home. The children especially liked him because he brought them bubble gum, and after all, he lived above Dipper Dans, an ice-cream parlor. He later married and set up practice in Toledo, Ohio. Each year, we have received Christmas cards with pictures of his two attractive daughters. We always have dinner with him when he comes back to Nashville for a Meacham Society meeting. From the very first of his training in India, he admired the work ethics of Dr. George Burrus and looked upon him as his mentor.

Colorful saris and good friend.

During his work at the hospital in Nadiad, George became very concerned that the hallway by surgery was always full of people and dogs. Also, the windows of surgery had no screens, and they seemed to him to be very easy situations to correct. He asked some hospital carpenters to close up the hallway, an act that upset the three American nurses who had been on the mission field for almost thirty years. George felt that from time to time changes were necessary, and fellow workers seemed very intent on maintaining the status quo. From time to time, they would bring up the concept of expediting the transfer of the hospital from foreign missionary care to care by the nationals. A difference of opinion became the foundation of working with the "ladies," and I have often wondered how the situation would have been resolved if we had not come home because of Ellen's illness.

During the writing of my book, I found a box of letters written to my mother and two sisters from India. Mother had saved the letters, which were lost for many years, and when I read them again, I realized their value in telling my story and my true feelings at the time about the events.

Monday
Aug. 13, 1962

Dearest Mother, Edwyna, & Gayle,

Well this is the first letter that I write you from Nadiad. We only arrived yesterday morning about 5:00 a.m. Our last week at sea was very rough, not only from the standpoint of rough water, but Laurie, Roger, and Kate all contracted chicken-pox. We had to go into ship quarantine for the second time and all three have had hard cases and look terrible in the face. Lisa's case was very light. You can imagine landing in Bombay with a crowd like this plus an eye infection that I had contacted a few days before. Dr. & Mrs. Aldrich, whose place we take, met us and it took George 5 hr. to get through Customs office. Bombay is very modern in parts with still traditional Indian stores and buildings. The saris that the women wear are very colorful, and I saw some beautiful pure silk material, all shades, that I'll bring you when we come home. We only stayed in Bombay one day and night before catching the train for Nadiad the evening of the 11th. We slept on the train and arrived about 5:00 a.m. Sunday morning. A large crowd of hospital staff, other missionaries, etc. met us at the station with garlands of beautiful fresh flowers. We were presented at a formal reception after church yesterday with more bouquets and garlands of roses, then early this morning a ceremony at the hospital with more garlands of flowers. This is their custom of greeting. Of course we didn't understand one word of the speeches but their faces conveyed their feelings of sincere welcome and interest in the new "Sahib" and "Madam Sahib." We shook hand after hand at all three garland ceremonies. George even went to work less than five hours after we arrived. He is so restless to be back at work. This six-week journey taxed us both and we are anxious to lead normal home and work lives again. However, I won't get to move into our home for about 3 more weeks. We are staying with Ola and Jim McClendon, the other young doctor & wife (internist). Their house is large and they have two small boys. We had a tour of the future Burrus "hotel" and it will take a letter to describe it. It is indeed monstrous! Even two full size dining rooms, kitchens, six or eight bedrooms, I can't remember which, very pretty garden with concrete pool and tea house (open on all four sides) and stone patios for the children to play and ride. Also one enormous screened in verandah upstairs and porches downstairs. Space I have! We have a cook, ayah (maid & baby sitter), gardener, and night watchman. Maybe a sweeper if we decide to use him. It will take time to get used to some of these strange customs, sights, and ideas & language so we'll have to take it day by day. Enjoyed the letters that were waiting for us and take care of yourselves. Swan had another girl. Gayle: I'll want details of Mar. 16th plans! Love to you all,

Barbara & Geo.

December 28, 1962

Dearest Edwyna & family,

We received your letter yesterday, and we too felt a lonesome feeling being away at the Christmas season. I thought about you all Christmas night here since it was Christmas morning there and I tried to picture Johnny and Jimmy discovering Santa Claus toys! I am glad that Mimi and Gayle were with you all that morning!

Before I tell you about our Christmas in India, let me thank you for the books that you sent us. Your box was the only one that arrived and everyone enjoyed opening their pretty wrapped package. George thoroughly enjoyed his book and completed it in two days, the 25th & 26th. He laughed out several times while reading it so I know he liked it. Laura liked her Huckleberry Hound book.

We made decorations for our Christmas tree during school hours the week before and used a tree out of our back yard. It wasn't a pine or cedar, but it looked quite nice after we finished it. Christmas Eve we all had dinner and sang carols down at Dr. McClendon's house. There were four missionary families in all, eight children, and the children were surprised by a visit from Santa Claus. One of the daddies had a real suit and popped in to distribute gifts. Roger went wild! Lisa only had a big grin since she had informed me a few days ago about the score on Santa Claus! Christmas morning we went to church services and for lunch we had some of the Indian interns and residents that were on duty during Christmas and couldn't go home. One of the boys was a Hindu so he wouldn't touch the turkey. (You know they don't eat meat!) We received many beautiful cards, some from people that we had never met, but who were interested in our work here. Some sent money for the hospital work which was of course welcomed! I am looking forward to the baby clothes that you are sending and appreciate the trouble it takes to pack and mail them. The rubber pants will be needed since Kate has about used hers to threads. She is getting to be quite a big girl, almost 2 yr. and follows Roger everywhere. George has had two good hunting days recently and killed about four black bucks so we have a good supply of meat. Write soon.

Love,

Barbara

Dec. 30th
Nadiad, India

Dearest Mother & Gayle,

Hope this letter finds you both well and relaxing from a happy, but busy Christmas season. I heard from Edwyna a few days ago and she told me about the ring and the breakfast to announce the engagement. Please keep me informed on all the doings because I will miss so much being a part of them.

Our first Christmas in India was as normal as could be expected since children anywhere make Christmas exciting! Christmas Eve about four missionary families got together for a dinner and party around the tree. One of the daddies had a real Santa Claus suit and when he appeared Roger and Kate went wild! Of course she does everything that he does so she was only mocking him!

Christmas Day we had Santa Claus about 6:30 and the girls got dolls, while Roger got a rifle pop gun! George has promised to take him out in the woods hunting. After breakfast we went to church services next door, and they lasted for 2 hr. all in the Gujurati language. We are picking up some of the language, and the children know some too. All day long there was a steady stream of people at the door, some to bring us Indian "sweets," Indian bands to play their weird music, friends to wish us a happy Christmas, and as usual beggars for money or food. As we were going to bed Christmas night I thought about you all just getting up to open packages with the Griscoms. I bet Johnny & Jimmy were excited! By the way have you ever received some Indian bedspreads? Also a magazine subscription to *Ladies' Home Journal*? Let me know! We received some Christmas cards from friends, and then some from people over the states that we didn't know. Some sent money to be used at the hospital which was greatly appreciated.

George operated on his first case of leprosy yesterday and has been unusually busy the past few days. Getting home for lunch at 4:00 p.m. etc. We enjoyed fixing Christmas for the servants and their families. About 35 in all so we fixed decorated boxes of fruit, candies, coconuts etc. for each family, some toys for the smaller kids, and material for pants, shirts, and dresses for the gardener, watchman, cook, and two ladies that help in the house. Please write us soon!

Love,

Barbara

Jan. 15, 1963

Dearest Mimi & Gayle,

Guess you two girls are deep in wedding plans, only wish that I could be there to get in on the talk! This letter finds us all well and busy with school, language study, and daily doings! I wish that you could see Katie now. She, of course, has changed more than any of the rest in the past 6 mo. and is very blonde with big blue eyes. She and Roger would pass for twins if he were not about a head taller. They walk around holding hands often and sometimes he refers to her as "naughty Katie." (Pot calling the kettle black!)

You mentioned a Christmas box in your last letter. Well it hasn't arrived, but remember that it takes a full 2 mo. so don't worry. I'll let you know when it arrives, and we'll appreciate it of course.

I'm having twenty-five in for dinner tomorrow night. George's surgical resident got married during Christmas and came back this week with his new wife. She is a doctor also and will work at the hospital. So we will have a dinner for them. Since the guest list will be part American and part Indian we'll have an Indian dinner of chicken, currey and rice plus the trimmings. I will admit that your menu for Gayle's breakfast sounded so good that I could almost taste it. I'll have to wait five years for food like that!

We had a unique experience yesterday. Jan. 14th is Kite Day all over India and has been observed for hundreds of years. One of the Hindu doctors in Nadiad invited us up to his house to watch the town's kites from his roof porch. In Nadiad shops are the ground floor in the bazaar while people live upstairs for 2 or 3 stories high. Then on top of the building is a roof porch. It was a beautiful sight when we reached the top because kites of all colors & shapes & sizes were in the sky! George and the children really enjoyed flying kites and Mama enjoyed the tea that was served to us.

I marvel everyday at George's strength in beginning chest work here and in mounting other obstacles that have come his way. Be sure to send us Gayle's picture and all the write-ups.

Love to you both,

Barbara

Jan. 27, 1963

Dearest Mother & Gayle,

I know that you girls are busy, but drop me a line about the plans, picture, parties, and etc. Who is going to be in the wedding and what have you bought for your trousseau? Here I sit halfway around the world and my curiosity is getting the best of me!

The children are all well and waiting for that "new baby" to come in a few weeks. One day they want a boy, then a girl, then twins! Katie is talking quite well, and everything now is "my." She is so blond that sometimes her hair looks white! Her eyes are very blue but maybe this next one will be a brown-eyed one!

My dinner for the Indian bride and groom turned out real well, and yesterday we had a picnic with some Americans living about 25 miles away. They drove over in the morning and stayed until about 9:00 last night.

School for Lisa and the little McClendon boy is coming along very well and the whole family is proud of the schoolroom. We have added a 4 ft. by 3 ft. abacus to use in counting, a bulletin board that is about 8 ft. by 5 ft. for the pictures, etc. and a blackboard about 4 ft. by 3 ft. Our next project is a sand table for the school. Lisa reads well and I would put her up to any Eakin School first grader right now. Hope she continues to be so interested. Laura knows where everything is in the school and all that's going on! She sees that the teacher and Laura have a piece of fruit each morning for story time! My boy is getting quite big and has a dog, ball, or gun on his mind most of the time. At night when he gets ready for bed all sorts of things fall out of his pockets. One night he left a pile of rocks by his bed and during the night I stepped on them in my bare feet!!

It hardly seems possible that Jan. is almost over! George has been very busy since Christmas and has gotten some chest work started! Please write soon and take care of each other for me.

Love,

Barbara

After that Christmas of 1962 in India, we waited with anticipation for the birth of our fifth child during February 1963.

My thoughts to share with you about Ellen will seem very short and factual, but somehow these feelings are the hardest for me to relate, partly because they belong only to me, and partly because they are too much of a mystery to explain, even to myself.

We chose the morning of February 21 for Ellen's birth. Everything at the hospital was ready and sterile for her delivery. George delivered Ellen, and we were relieved at how smooth it all took place. The other four children were delighted with her birth, and for many weeks, we played with and rejoiced in our new addition.

Feb. 21, 1963

Dearest Mimi, Edwyna & Gayle,

Well Roger is surrounded by girls! Our fourth girl, Ellen, was born this afternoon at 1:30 p.m. She weighed 8 lb. 8 oz. and has the distinction of being delivered by her father. She is 19 in. long and very chubby. She looks very much like Laura did as a baby. The other four are very excited over her, and George brought them over tonight to see her.

She has been in my room now since birth and will stay in here the whole time that I'm in the hospital. This will be a new experience having her in the room with me all the time.

George and I left home about 7:30 and walked to hospital. They started a drip about 8:30 and things progressed until 1:30! She seems quite healthy and we are so pleased with her!

Please write soon and keep us informed on the wedding plans and pieces in the paper! Our love to Johnny G. and Jimmy and better close since I've had sort of a busy day (ha).

Love from us all,

Barbara, George, Lisa, Laura, Roger, Kate, Ellen

March 8, 1963

Dearest Edwyna,

I'm sure by now you know about our Ellen born Feb. 21st at 1:30 p.m. She weighed 8 lb. and looks much like Laura did as a baby, dark hair and eyes. George and I left home about 7:30 that morning and he started a drip about 8:30. He delivered her and yelled "Choori" when she was born. This is the Indian word for girl and everyone in the delivery room got a kick out of this! We are so thankful for her and her health. Even with two big sisters and two little sisters, Roger still seems able to take care of himself! He's going through a phase now of only wanting to wear "pocket pants" and "pocket shirts." He keeps them filled with rocks, and candy when he can get it! I started breast feeding Ellen but had to stop a few days ago when I developed a breast infection. Feel better today, however!

How are wedding plans coming? I know that Gayle is getting excited and everyone is very busy! Please be sure to send me any pictures or paper clippings that come out.

I've been home from the hospital a week now and things are running fairly smooth. The kids found a big turtle outside today so it's now in one of the downstairs bathrooms in a large tub. I don't know how long I'll be able to stand it there!

Some American friends close by sent us some bacon and ham yesterday so it was a real experience to wake up and smell bacon frying this morning and to taste baked ham for supper tonight! The first bacon and ham we've had since July 1st! These friends are with some American construction co. and they keep them well supplied with home products.

With five little ones, I must confess I enjoy having a cook! He comes every day at 6:00 a.m. and usually stays until 7:00 or 7:30 p.m. at night. He goes home between 1:30 and 4:00. My two women helpers in the house are very good and have been a great help especially now! Write us soon, and give our love to John & the boys.

Love,

Barbara

March 17, 1963

Dearest Gayle,

Well the big day is drawing near, and I'm sure you are both excited and busy at the same time. We will all be thinking of you and I know you will be a pretty bride. It will be Sunday morning here when you marry, and I'll try to picture everything.

Ellen continues to grow and do well. She looks like Laura did as a baby. We had to change her to a bottle as I had a breast infection and couldn't go on nursing her. The other four all stand around when she's having her bath or taking a bottle and if someone comes to the door for a visit they take him straight to Ellen's bed.

Roger will be three the 22nd and Kate will be two on your birthday the 27th. Roger is very rough at times and has knocked out one of his front teeth. I hate it because it will be two or three years before his permanent one comes in! He asks "why" all day long about everything he wears, does, or eats! Kate is a very sweet child and very independent. She is completely trained and can dress herself part way. She speaks half in English and half in Gujurati language. Lisa started back to school this past week and reads well for a first grader. Laura still tends to everyone in the house, and is getting quite grown-up in some ways.

Enough about my "five." I know that you will be too busy to answer this right away, but when you get settled in Fort Sill, write us your address and all about the wedding. Maybe mother can send me a paper clipping after the wedding.

Before I close I want to wish you all the happiness in the world, and hope that you will be as happy as I have been and are now. It's a give and take life and only this way can it last. Give our love to Jerry and remember we all love you.

Barbara

However, Ellen was not a well baby, and this soon became evident. She had many convulsions each day, and our first concern was getting her to Nashville for Dr. Amos Christie to see her. He was chief of the Department of Pediatrics at Vanderbilt for many years, and he was George's teacher in medical school. Many years later, some money from the Ellen Burrus Fund was given to him to use for his volunteer work at the Nashville Union Rescue Mission.

George, Roger, and Ellen left Nadiad in early April for the United States, and Lisa, Laura, Kate, and I remained in India, feeling sure of their return. Roger had some indications of tuberculosis, so he went home with George and Ellen for evaluation. The following letters will give you a picture of the five weeks to follow, during which time we were hopeful for Ellen's recovery. However, this was not the plan to be. George gave me permission to include these letters because they present a clear and precise record of our emotions at that time in our lives.

April 26, 1963

Dearest Mother,

I was so glad to hear from you last night and the report about Ellen! George was gone one week to the day before the Cablegram arrived saying he felt she would be alright and that was the hardest & longest week of my life. I got through it somehow, but am still anxiously awaiting a letter from him with details and news! After his plane left the ground I felt that we had made the wrong decision for the girls and I to stay here, however, maybe we did the right thing. I knew George was the one to go since he could understand the medical terms and procedures, but it was hard to see my baby of two months go so far. I hope by now that you've seen Roger and will no doubt see a big change in him in almost a year.

After being very busy everyday with five children, the drop to three left me some spare time. I've tried to concentrate on school routine for Lisa and some extra attention for Laura and Kate.

George is very much missed here by the Indian people as well as by us girls, and many have come by to see us and ask about him. I must confess that India loses its "charm" without the rest of the family.

The hot season of 100° to 115° is here and I keep the girls inside from about 10:00 in the morning until 5:30 in the afternoon. This tropical sun makes Houston weather seem mild!

Don't you think that Ellen favors Laura as a baby? Or do you remember? I only hope and pray that she's alright and that George can bring her home soon. Please write soon with news about seeing them. Hope this letter finds you well and rested from the wedding. I appreciated the clippings!

All my love,

Barbara

April 7, 1963

Dear Mama, Lisa, Laura, Kate,

I certainly enjoyed the letter from all my girls. I love each one of you. Everybody here is just fine and we're all hoping Baby Ellen is going to be alright. So far the L.P., EEG and routine lab studies have all been normal. Dr. Christie is concerned that she still is having the convulsions without him being able to find a definite cause. Ellen is in the Nursery on the Pediatric floor where it is air conditioned and where there are constant attendants. I go out to see her every day and hold her but I don't stay with her all the time. She is on Similac and takes it well. Dr. Christie said to tell you that she is continuing to gain weight and is a happy baby. He wants to watch her however for a while before he makes his mind up about letting me bring her back to India. Roger's tests so far have been negative except for a (+) histoplasmin skin test. The histoplasmin complement fixation test is not back yet. Let Jim check the mess cook account unless he wants you to do it. Also let Jim know about Ellen and also give my regards to everyone. For the present time I think our decision for you to stay has been right and we'll just have to wait and see how everything is going to turn out.

I've been keeping all the kin folks informed about Ellen and have seen everybody except Baba & Mama Howard. I hate to leave town till Ellen is out of the hospital. I'm going to buy a Volkswagen car and try to bring it home with me. If I can't then I'll just sell it to Swan. I think we need transportation in Nadiad and I think you can learn to drive the bug.

Roger and I think of you all the time. He and I eat ice cream for you every day. We also ride the ponies every day.

I have talked to the church at Hendersonville twice and will talk to Inglewood and West End. Dr. & Mrs. Freeman called from Houston to learn about Ellen. I surely appreciated their concern. I'll keep you informed and you look after the bunnies and yourself. I love all of you all—especially Mama.

Love,

The Boys

May 1, 1963

Dearest Barbara,

I know things are worrying you because Ellen is sick. So far we haven't come up with the diagnosis and it looks like we might not be able to diagnose it. I know this will worry you but Dr. Christie is very concerned that he can't find a cause. He is afraid this may mean that our baby is going to be very sick. The bad thing is that there may be nothing medically that we can do. He is having Dr. Meacham see Ellen to see if he feels that further diagnostic studies are indicated. I will keep you informed of any further developments.

I myself feel that our decision to be a medical missionary was the right decision and continues to be the right decision. If Dr. Christie feels that Ellen can go back to India no matter what the outcome then I think I ought to bring her back. If he feels that she should stay here for awhile then I think she should stay here. There are several possibilities and I'll do what you feel is best since as you know the family comes first. If Ellen needs to stay here then I would like to bring you all home and then I would go back for awhile. Perhaps by six months things would be more clear. Of course all of us could stay here. I'm sure there may be other choices that you can suggest. Also the board may have some suggestions.

Roger is doing fine, eating well and gaining weight.

I go to the hospital daily to hold Ellen and love her. She is gaining weight and except for an occasional jerk seems perfectly healthy. I hope and pray that this isn't as bad as I have intimated but you wanted to know everything and I feel like you should know everything.

Again let me say that my first concern is to my God, next to my family. I'm sure no matter what happens we will continue to be true to Him and our family.

My love for you grows daily and I wish we could be together during this difficulty.

All the family sends their love and prayers.

Love,

George

Send me the address of Dr. Aldrich so I can pay him for the deep freeze. Also send Swan the title for the car. Also be sure to cancel the dental appointments, etc.

May 3, 1963

Dearest Mama,

Things are pretty much stable as far as Ellen is concerned. She remains in the hospital under close observation. I fed her a bottle of milk today and she looked happy and smiled for me. She continues to eat well. There are no further developments in the case and Dr. Christie hasn't said what we should do.

I carried Roger out to Marianne's today to spend a couple of days. He and Dan play so well together. I will spend the night over there tomorrow night and then bring him back to Hendersonville. He continues to eat well and is happy. He is really eating the chewing gum.

I went out to Vanderbilt today and watched Hal Collins do an open heart operation. Things went well and it looks like Hal is getting off to a good start.

I'm going to try to bring back a Volkswagen ambulance which we will be able to use for some trips. I hope you will be able to drive and go visit in Baroda, etc.

I've been out to see Edwyna and her two boys. They both look good.

Keep looking after yourself and the girls. As always I can't see the hills—especially with a sick baby. I'm sure the Bishop feels that the hills will help us but I doubt it.

I might be able to get some shoes at a bargain price. Does anybody need any? I don't know how much I'll be able to bring back since I don't have too much poundage but send the lists as they come to your mind and I'll do my best. What size dress do you want?

Love,

Daddy, Roger, Ellen

Please send Dr. Aldrich's address so I can send him a check for the deep freeze.

May 8, 1963

Dearest Barbara, Lisa, Laura & Kate,

Daddy sure does miss you all way over there in Nadiad. I'm beginning this letter at Poppi's and will finish it after we talk to Dr. Christie. We've been out to dinner at the Reynolds and the Regens. I talked at West End Sunday and will go out to Dr. Isenhour's tonight. The response to our work has been grand. I have heard from Dr. Freeman and from Hank but everything is just hanging till I find out how Ellen is going to do.

Roger and I went fishing and he caught two fish. I went fishing this morning with Gene Gober but only got nibbles.

I've been working in the yard and getting a little tan. I'm feeling good and eating too much. I have been driving Sonny's car which has been very convenient. I'm getting the Volkswagen today so that will save us money. You might as well go ahead and learn to drive so you can go to Anand, etc. with the children.

Well Ellen is home now and doing fine. Dr. Christie remains pessimistic about her but says there is a chance she'll grow out of it. He feels that she will probably be alright to make the trip back to Nadiad. I will send a medical report to the Board of Missions and talk with them.

I'm getting anxious to see all the bunnies and Mama.

The weather here is just perfect. I've been cutting grass and pulling up stumps. I'm hoping that we'll be home in about two weeks if everything works out well.

I love you,

George

May 11, 1963

Dearest Barbara, Lisa, Laura & Kate,

Baby Ellen is doing fine and eating well at Poppi's and will stay at Marianne's in a few days. I will carry Roger down to Franklin and Columbia in a few days. I've written letters to the Board saying we're ready to return and am awaiting their reply. I've also written Dr. Freeman saying I would be glad to come to Houston for a visit.

Roger and I are going over to Billy Hitts for a swim today.

I carried the little Volkswagen to the shop today to get the stretcher built in. I've written Harold Olson about shipping instructions.

I have talked with Ben St. Clair and Dr. Hillman about the long-range plan of medical missions and about our mission itself. We are scheduled to have a talk with Bishop Short next Monday. I believe someone must at least inform the Church concerning the problems of medical missions. I hesitated to sort of go around the Board but feel that this may be the better approach. I know the Board knows my feelings on the subject. I've told Hank & Dr. Brewster that I would come to New York to talk if they felt this would be beneficial.

I'm still working in the yard and am getting quite a sun burn.

Ellen had another convulsion tonight after I started this letter. At the present time she is on sedation. She hadn't had a convulsion for about two weeks. I wonder how you would feel about coming home and letting me return to Nadiad for awhile. Would you be able to look after our little brood without daddy?

My first concern is Ellen and the family but I also hate to leave the hospital without a surgeon if you felt you could take care of things here.

As you can see I don't really know what is the best thing to do. It may be that the Board will make some of the decisions for us.

Anyway I love you and want to know what you think should be done.

Love,

Daddy

All of these letters explain the anxiety and concern that we experienced for the five weeks that I remained in India with Lisa, Laura, and Kate. I tried to keep on an even keel, so one day I took off for an excursion away from Nadiad.

We had some American friends and patients who were working on a dam in Duvaran, India. Leaving the girls with our ayah, Ruth, I went to visit them. When I returned late that night, Ruth was all upset about something and kept repeating "fire, fire," one of her few English words. She handed me a note from the American internist, Jim McClendon, who explained that two-year-old Kate had burnt the bottom of both feet while walking over hot coals. The Indians build small fires everywhere and brew their tea. Jim said to bring Kate to the hospital the next day for treatment and new bandages. We went twice a day for about three weeks, and we called her feet "Mickey Mouse" because of the thick bandages.

After five weeks, I received the following letter from George:

Dearest Barbara,

I hope the cable doesn't cause you any worry. In talking with the Board of Missions in New York, we have decided that you and the children should come home and that I should stay here and get you settled. After this I will return to Nadiad and continue the work. I particularly want you to discuss Ellen's health with Dr. Christie and get everything straight in your mind before I leave.

I know there are many details that you will have to work out in leaving, but I know you will be able to do these and I hope rapidly. As far as the house is concerned, lock it up and make sure Jim knows I will be back in a week or two. Continue Cordabhi and Ruth until I get there, but go ahead and let Mirium go back to work for the hospital. Make arrangements for paying these two before you leave.

I am including the passports as you see and as you probably know, you will have to clear with the Police and the Internal Revenue office, and get a No Objection return permit for you and the children before you leave. I am sure that Jim and Bob Davies, and also Dr. Sigal, can help you with these as they helped me. As I am sure you know, Dr. Sigal has close contacts with the folks at the mill and can get things done in India where you and I can't get them done.

I have talked with Hank and he has said that the Board of Missions will pay for the plane tickets. Go ahead and contact IMBO and either let them buy round the world tickets from Ahmedabad, or give you a guarantee and let you buy the tickets in Ahmedabad. Be sure to buy this type ticket as it will be cheaper when you return. Of course, you can always cancel this ticket if it becomes necessary, but once you fly one way, you won't get the discount. As you remember with Bob Davies help, I got out in three days. The rush is not on so it is not necessary for you to get out in this length of time, but I would push right along and not let yourself be caught up in red tape. If you aren't careful the IMBO office may be hesitant and unknowingly try to delay you. If this is the case, go around them and get on out of there.

Be sure to let Jim help you with all the required shots, etc. Write me as soon as things are worked out; or if you get things worked out quickly, just cable me when to meet you in Nashville.

I might reiterate that the trip is right pleasant once you get on the plane at Bombay. Of course there will be some lay over in Bombay but you can handle this. I would also notify Hank Lacey's office in New York either by letter or cable when you arrive there and someone from the Board will probably meet you and help you through Customs.

I hope this has mentioned all points about which you might have some concern. Again let me assure you that Ellen is all right.

Love,

George
GB:w

May 14, 1963

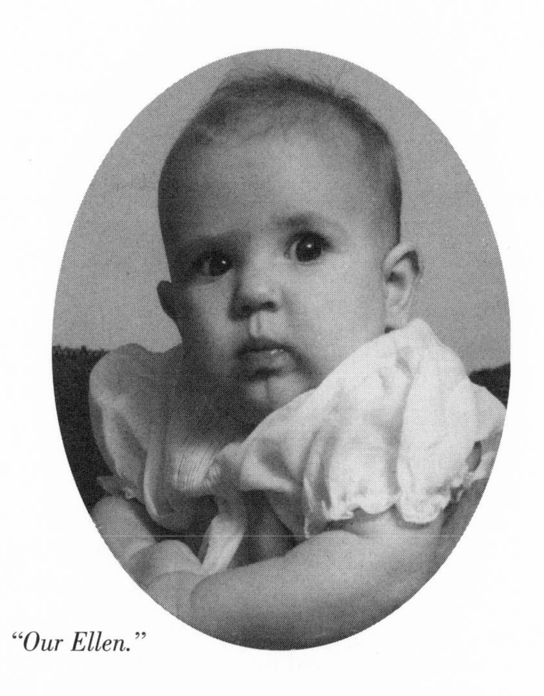

"Our Ellen."

I did work hard on our return, but it still took me a week to get out of India and past the red tape. The girls and I left the country late one afternoon and started our journey from Ahmadabad to Nashville, Tennessee, halfway around the world! Before I left India, I really felt that we would be returning, so I left some money in the bank and all my wedding china, crystal, and gold leaf mirror in the house. As Cordabhi walked to the car with us, I said, "We'll be back as soon as possible." He replied, "No, you will never return." He spoke the truth.

After extensive investigation by the Department of Pediatrics, Dr. Bertram Sprofkin, who was one of George's teachers in neurology, and Dr. Christie felt that Ellen had Schilder's disease, a demyelinating disease. The treatment was mainly symptomatic with control of the convulsions as the main objective. This turned out to be quite difficult, and the overall prognosis was not good.

Ellen was with us for four years. I will never understand the "why" of it all, except one truth I learned; when you need the strength to carry on, God sends that strength to you. Maybe the following poem will help:

HEAVEN'S VERY SPECIAL CHILD

A meeting was held quite far from earth
"It's time again for another birth,"
Said the Angels to the Lord above,
"This special child will need much love.

"His progress may seem very slow,
Accomplishments he may not show,
And he'll require extra care
From the folks he meets way down there.

"He may not run or laugh or play
His thoughts may seem quite far away,
In many ways he won't adapt,
And he'll be known as handicapped.

"So let's be careful where he's sent
We want his life to be content.
Please, Lord, find the parents who
Will do a special job for You.

"They will not realize right away
The leading role they're asked to play,
But with this child sent from above
Comes stronger faith and richer love.

"And soon they'll know the privilege given
In caring for this gift from Heaven,
Their precious charge, so meek and mild
Is Heaven's very special child!"

—Author Unknown

Our doctor and friend, Dr. Amos Christie.

Ellen never walked or talked, but we loved and took good care of her, hoping somehow that she felt our presence. She convulsed two or three times every day for four years.

When Ellen was two years old, Nan was born and brought extra joy to our lives. Two years later at Ellen's death, Nan was my salvation, since the older four went to school and two-year-old Nan was very active at home. For a few days, she looked and looked for "our baby."

After Ellen's death in May 1967, we established the Ellen Burrus Fund. It was our way of making funds available to be used for children's health research or for any projects related to actual mental or physical needs of children. Our good friend and pastor of West End United Methodist Church in Nashville, Rev. Ben B. St. Clair, helped us lay the groundwork for this endeavor. In a small way, this fund helped to answer the "why" for George and me.

We were never able to return to India, and Dr. and Mrs. McClendon packed up our goods. All of my china and crystal made the trip back; however, my gold leaf mirror graces some home, large or small, somewhere in the world.

After we returned from India, our family settled in Nashville close to family and friends. We chose to live in an area close to the hospital, a good neighborhood school, Woodmont Elementary, and our church,

The family—before Ellen's death and Barbara's birth.

West End United Methodist. We bought a house on Golf Club Lane and have been there for some thirty-three years. The name of the street was easy for friends near and far to remember over the years.

Before going to India, we were commissioned at St. Paul's United Methodist Church in Houston, Texas, by Bishop Paul Martin. This church and West End United Methodist Church in Nashville were part of our support in India. Therefore, we have been a part of West End's worship, activities, and support for some thirty-three years. I enjoyed ten years of playing handbells at West End under an exceptional musician, Don Marler. The following paper was written as advent thoughts in the West End Advent Book:

> Many things enter our thoughts as we approach the Advent season. It is difficult to filter out the best from all the good that flows in the mainstream of the holiday celebration. Each year as we

await the celebration of the birth of the Christ Child, the activities at the church, at home, and the schools crowd into the already bulging routine of daily activities.

In Bosobe, Zaire, where we served in a small "bush" community with the church, hospital and school as the center of our lives, life moved at a slower pace. We did not have to worry about cars and those things utilizing electricity. Rushing to the supermarket, picking up the children after school, ball practice, or piano lessons were not an issue.

As we worked in the maternity section of the small hospital, Barbara and I marveled at the young mothers who came for delivery. Many came long distances, always by foot or carried on a stretcher or bicycle. They might stay several weeks awaiting delivery and would sleep in the small rooms and cook over an outside fire. Following delivery they wrapped their babies in very simple clothing to protect them from the heat, mosquitoes, and flies. They tended to their every need and look forward with anticipation as they began to grow.

> *He will feed his flock like a shepherd, he will gather the lambs in his arms, he will carry them in his bosom, and gently lead those that are with young. (Isa. 40:11)*

We knew that these little bundles of humanity were in extreme danger since by the age of two approximately half of them would succumb to malaria, measles, pneumonia, and other maladies. It was difficult for us to understand and to accept this loss of infant life, but we understood the mother's love. Certainly the God who brought the Christ Child to Bethlehem's manger, who breathes life into the babes born in the bush, and who seemingly cares for all of us at West End as if we are his very own, will help our world to understand his message of love—a message that is inclusive, unfailing and that holds us in his arms as it held the Babe in Bethlehem and the babes in Bosobe.

George Burrus

The family—before the adventure of Africa.

George's future partners, Bill Stoney and Bill Alford, had been in medical school and part of residency with him, and in 1963, they started the heart surgery team at St. Thomas Hospital in Nashville. The group now includes twelve cardiothoracic surgeons.

Our Nan was born in 1965, Ellen died in 1967, and Barbara was born in 1968. Golf Club Lane was a part of their lives from the beginning and our memories of Ellen's four years.

In 1968, George, Dr. Bill Stoney, Dr. Bill Alford, Dr. Harry Page, and Dr. Geoffrey Berry flew to Cape Town, South Africa, to observe the work of Dr. Christian Barnard, who had performed the first human heart transplant about a month earlier, and the second transplant about a week earlier. I later met Dr. Barnard when I accompanied George to a thoracic meeting in Toronto, Canada. Much later he visited Nashville and the facilities at St. Thomas Hospital.

CHAPTER 3

Bosobe and Kinshasa, Zaire

Africa, 1969–1971

We had been home from India about six years when George again started to talk about the mission field and the pull he felt toward "being a doctor where there was no doctor." George contacted LAOS (Layman's Overseas Service), an agency in Mississippi that coordinates people to places for mission work. They replied that a doctor was needed for a Swedish Baptist Hospital in central Zaire. The family said that I could veto the idea. However, I was not going to grow old with George and have him regret that he did not return to the mission field. We talked to Dr. Ruden, a representative of the Swedish Baptist Church, plans were made, and the next thing that I realized was that I was packing up six children, my husband, and myself for two years of service in deep, dark Africa. Lisa was twelve, Laura was eleven, Roger was nine, Kate was eight, Nan was four, and Barbara was nine months old.

We wanted to keep our house if possible, and the opportunity presented itself when Rev. and Mrs. Frank Calhoun, parents of Marianne Burrus, needed a home in Nashville. Rev. Calhoun had married George and me in 1953, and his first pastorate had been in Thompson Station, Tennessee. My grandparents, Mr. and Mrs. John

Our household in Brussels, ready to study French!

Edward Howard Jr., were in his first congregation.

Since French was the common language spoken in the mission, we were sent to Brussels, Belgium, for six months of language study. George had studied French at Vanderbilt, but Spanish and German had been my choices, so you can imagine my difficulty living in Brussels and running a household.

We arrived in Brussels, Belgium early one morning in July 1969. We were met by an American couple employed by the Swedish Baptists and taken to a typical Belgium row house in the suburbs. The house had four floors counting the basement, and each floor was about twenty-five feet wide. Because of jet lag, we all immediately went to bed, and hours later, I woke up to the sound of the "ice cream" man playing jingle bells! For a few minutes, I wondered just where I was.

The family settled in very well, and we enjoyed being able to walk to the bakery, flower shop, grocery, and laundry. Years later, we returned twice to the neighborhood to reminisce and visit the stores. Lisa and Laura attended St. Trinity Catholic Girls' School in the city and caught a bus in front of the house. Sometimes George would take them to school on his way downtown to the Institute of French Studies. He attended classes four days a week to study French in preparation for his work in Zaire.

Kate and Roger walked to the neighborhood French school, and they adjusted quite well. However, when the teacher sent home a note in French, I took it next door to Hans VanDenbrock, an interpreter for the Common Market. Nan tried out a French kindergarten, but did not like bowing and kissing the teacher on both cheeks. Barbara stayed at home with me.

The children were all good sports about the language problems. We used our television as a means of studying French. Twice a week we had family French lessons around the dining room table. Our teacher was a patient and kind lady of Polish origin named Madame Ruffkash. You can imagine how well I could concentrate with a nine month old in the playpen, plus trying to make my very southern accent sound like a French accent!

My favorite place to visit in Brussels was the Grand-Place, a square surrounded by old medieval buildings and the center of flower shows and lace shopping. Years later, I would purchase a wedding veil for my five daughters in the Grand-Place in Brussels.

Every Thursday when the lesson was over, we packed up and went for a long weekend camping trip somewhere in Europe. For example, we camped in Germany next to the Wall, and we went through Check Point Charlie into East Berlin. Other weekends we spent in France, Austria, Liechtenstein, the Netherlands, and Switzerland. We had a Volkswagen Combi, and all eight of us slept inside. Later, we bought a three-room tent, which was a real chore for the children to assemble.

We watched Neil Armstrong's landing on the moon, and later we would meet the astronaut in Kinshasa, Zaire.

One of our favorite side trips was to Brugge, Belgium, the lace-making center of the world. It was fascinating to watch the older women sit beside the canals and tat their lace.

Our last trip from Belgium was to Sweden and Denmark to once again talk to the Swedish Baptist executive secretary, Sven Ohm. It was in Stockholm, Sweden, that Barbara took her first step at age one. We spent a week in Stockholm and made a day's trip to Uppsala, Sweden, to visit Dr. Buckstrum. Dr. Buckstrum had spent some years in Boshwe,

Zaire, and had plans to return. We were invited to his home for dinner and enjoyed the authentic Swedish meatballs. I invited his wife to come back to Zaire with him for a visit. She did not answer, only smiled in a rather peculiar way. I learned later that she had had her appendix removed on their kitchen table in Boshwe, with her husband as the surgeon. No wonder she was not very enthusiastic about a return visit! After dinner, we were taken to view some Viking graves. These were ten-foot mounds of dirt and a prime tourist attraction in Uppsala. The following letters are my observations of Brussels at that time:

June 19, 1969
Bruxelles, Belgium

Dear Mother and Bob,

Well we made the trip reasonably well with everyone doing their share of helping and fussing! We arrived in Bruxelles about 11:00 a.m. and found that we had a place ready for us to live. (My phone just rang and it gives you a most peculiar feeling to answer and have someone start speaking French a mile a minute!) Our living quarters are quite adequate for the few months that we will be here. It's a house but each house connects to the other one and consists of three floors. Therefore they are narrow with two floors above the entrance. Our front yard has an iron gate then nothing but roses to the front door—no grass! The back yard has a lovely garden with roses and small fish pond. However, the kitchen is only big enough for one person at a time with a gas (ugh) stove. On the first floor we have a long entrance hall, kitchen, dining room, and 2 parlors. On the 2nd floor 2 bedrooms, and a bath, and on the 3rd floor 2 bedrooms. (Roger & Lisa stay up here.)

You would have enjoyed seeing my trip to the grocery store today. French labels and strange things to eat plus a different money standard. I tried to communicate in my way, but as we left the store Laura said I embarrassed her too much! We are in walking distance of a drug store, 2 or 3 groceries, laundromat, school, & post office.

The kids are already trying out French on each other. Barbara was a pretty good traveler, and slept well on the planes. However, I have never been as tired in my 37 years as I was yesterday upon arriving. However, I feel somewhat better today. Better close and get to bed. We are having trouble getting adjusted to the time change (we are 5 hrs. ahead of you) and the little ones are sleeping more in the day than night. Write us soon.

Love,

Barbara & "family"

June 30, 1969
Bruxelles, Belgium

Dear Mother & Bob,

I have so much to tell that I hardly know where to begin! First of all we received your letter a few days ago, and it was good to hear from you. You asked me what George was doing, well he has been busy seeing about a car and T.V. set. We have purchased both. Most of the T.V. programs are in French so we felt that it would help us in learning some French (good excuse!).

We bought a blue V.W. bus that gives us plenty of room to travel in and even to sleep if necessary. Everyone was so excited last Friday when we got it that we all piled in and went for a short ride south of the city. We rode out to Waterloo and saw the monument of the Battle of Waterloo, where Napoleon and Wellington fought. Both Saturday and Sunday we took day long trips coming back home at night.

I suggest that you get a map of Europe and follow our trips each weekend. We plan to study French Monday through Thursday, then travel Friday, Sat., and Sunday. This will be our plan for the summer months. On Saturday we went to Brugge, the center of the lace making industry and also called the "Venice" of Northern Europe because of its canals and medieval buildings. We watched a little old lady make lace (fascinating) and then we took a boat trip over the city by way of the canals. The scenery was beautiful and we saw some buildings built in the 1600's. The lace clothes were beautiful!

Sunday we went to Ostend, a sea resort (the North Sea), and played some on the beach. Then on to Antwerp, the 3rd largest seaport in Europe. This is where George will study some from October to March. Then we headed north to Holland. We only went a little ways into Holland (Breda), but we still saw some windmills and etc. George has enjoyed seeing the farm lands along the way and I enjoy the flowers (beautiful!!). The kids enjoy eating, and making noise along the way! It almost takes steel nerves to travel with them all (George included!).

We are all going to study French with a teacher. She comes to the house at 8:30 a.m. From 8:30 to 9:30 she teaches George and the children. Then from 9:30 to 10:30 George and I have a lesson. With my southern drawl it's hard to pronounce!

We also purchased an iron and the children call me "Esther." However the big girls are ironing some and since I have no help outside the house everyone is doing their share. We walk one mile to wash, and they take turns carrying and etc. We have a kitchen schedule that works well (clearing the table, drying, and sweeping). However, someone is always trying to switch their duties!

Better close and check on the kids & Geo. They have headed for the bakery and I need to watch out for them! The homemade bread is excellent! However the walking to do my wash and shopping help with the calories.

Love,

Barbara

July 16, 1969
Bruxelles, Belgium

Dear Mother & Bob,

I am also taking advantage of writing while under the dryer. This is my second hair appointment and my French beauty operator is very good! We have just returned from a five day camping trip in Switzerland. Never before have I seen such marvelous scenery!! Words can't describe the snow-capped peaks of the Alps or the beautiful lakes at the foot of the mountains. We left Bruxelles last Friday and made our way to Aachen, Germany, then on to Strasbourg, France, and back into Germany. Since France, Germany, and Switzerland all border together you go in and out one country and then another! After Germany, we went through the Rhine Valley, a fertile lowlands beside the Rhine River. Here we saw the Rhine Falls, the largest in Europe & something like Niagara Falls. From here we went to Zurich, Switzerland, and over the mountain to St. Gotthard's Pass. At night we would camp by a lake at the foot of a snow peaked mountain. However, we drove up and the children played in the snow and climbed up the mountains. We all slept in the V.W. bus and now have decided we do need a tent! It certainly teaches each child to do his part when a family of eight camp & cook out under the stars for five days!!

We went on to Lucerne, Switzerland, and here we did some shopping. We bought an authentic Swiss cow bell (to call my bunch to a meal), a real cuckoo clock that is adorable. It has a band of musicians that play a tune on the hour and half hour after the bird comes out! Nan sits and waits for the cuckoo bird! It is a treasure for the whole family! George & Roger each got a real Swiss pocket knife with attachments and I got my dented copper baking dish (about 18 ins. long) that I had wanted since I saw the one Mrs. Niederhauser brought Mary Joyce back from Switzerland. It is lovely and you can cook in it as well as serve. We came home by way of Lucerne to Mulhouse, Nancy to Metz (all in France),

Luxembourg, and on to Bruxelles! (Follow your map!)

I will write more after I hear from you from Georgia. George took me out to a real French restaurant for my birthday and we had a five course meal: Ham, soup, shrimp, steak, & dessert! It was called "La Chalet de la Forest" and had atmosphere as well as good food. The children say hello to Bob and write us soon.

Love,

Barbara

Aug. 9, 1969
Bruxelles, Belgium

Dearest Mother & Bob,

I hope you all got our card from Germany. I think I used the wrong box number. We had a five day trip counting going and coming and two days in Berlin. It was an interesting city because of the new and old. In West Berlin they have rebuilt modern buildings to replace bombed ones, yet many old buildings & churches were untouched. It took quite a long time to get into East Germany (showing passports etc.) and then some more time to go past the Wall into East Berlin. I was surprised at the good condition of East Berlin (nice stores and etc.) but it's just the idea that these people we passed walking on the streets could not leave the city. That bothered me. They seemed content, but you couldn't tell what they felt or were thinking. I breathed easier when we went back into West Berlin! Our souvenir purchase in Germany was a pair of

"Hummel" figurines. They are made in Germany, but are sold all over the world. I am sure you have seen them. I was looking for a special one and finally found it. It was too expensive, but I can count it as birthday, Christmas, etc. The children enjoyed eating in an authentic German restaurant complete with band and were delighted when Mama and Daddy did the polka to one of the tunes! Everyone that is except Lisa, she turned her head!

School starts in about three weeks so we will have to curtail our travels somewhat. However, we want to go to Paris for a day and then maybe one more camping trip to Denmark and Sweden. George has to go to Sweden to meet with the board and I would like to see these countries.

I guess this will be our last letter to Georgia, so we'll wait for your North Carolina address. Roger remarked just today that Mimi was so "cooperative" to write us so much!

Gayle and Edwyna seem to be having a good summer swimming with their kids. Gayle wrote that Mrs. Jones had quit at the office. I know Dr. Sadler misses her.

Better close and fix some lunch for this crowd. I have fixed 3 meals a day all summer and I am ready for a break. However, our family has had a good summer of real "togetherness." Nobody has been going off in different directions. Write soon.

Our love,

Barbara & family

Sept. 26, 1969
Bruxelles, Belgium

Dear Family,

This will be our last letter from Belgium as we leave here next Thursday the 2nd of October for Kinshasa, Africa. We are going by plane and will go to Madrid, Spain, for four days, then on to Africa the 7th of Oct. We plan to see a bullfight in Madrid and enjoy the Spanish sunshine for a few days! Our trunks and car left by boat this week and will arrive in Africa the 12th of October. The children will go to school here through next Wednesday. Believe it or not they are all passing in the French school!

Here is our temporary address in Kinshasa:

Dr. George Burrus
Union Missionaire Hospitaliere
Boite Postale 658
Kinshasa
Republique Du Congo

We had a nice visit last week from Gloria Graves, my neighbor on Hampton Ave. at home. She came to Europe with her husband who is in the shoe import business and came to Bruxelles to see us and a Belgium friend. She stayed with the Belgium friend, but came over to see us twice. One day George and I took her about 25 miles to a small lace-making community that is very picturesque and quaint. We took a canal ride at twilight and ate at a lovely "old English inn." Another day I went out to lunch with Gloria and her friend. Guess who baby-sat! "The doctor himself." She is going to call Edwyna when she gets home Oct. 3rd.

Barbara walks all over the place and can be a little spit-fire from time to time. All of the others jump when she fusses or cries.

Have a letter waiting for us, and we'll send a card from Spain.

Our love,

Barbara

We left Brussels the first of October to fly to Kinshasa, Zaire, and begin our African adventure. Originally, we were supposed to spend a year in Brussels while we studied French and George took some tropical medicine courses in Antwerp, Belgium. He had met a young doctor in Belgium who had been able to go on to Africa earlier without taking the courses. The young doctor, Ron Tolls, and his wife, Jan, became our friends in Brussels, and George inquired how he was able to bypass the courses. He said that Dr. William Close, physician to President Mobutu of Zaire, had helped him, and George immediately contacted Dr. Close and asked the same favor.

Dr. Close, father of the American actress, Glenn Close, became a friend of ours, and when we met him in Kinshasa before we went up-country to Boshwe, he asked George to consider staying in Kinshasa and working for FOMECO (Foundation Medical Congo). The organization was formed to upgrade the country's health institutes, with the main hospital being in Kinshasa. It was named "Mama Yemo" after Mobutu's mother.

On the way to Africa, we stopped in Madrid, Spain, and enjoyed a few days of sightseeing in yet another culture. We especially liked the town of Toledo, famous for pottery, steel swords, and the Alcazar, the military academy of Spain. We attended a bullfight, but left early due to our distaste for the sport.

My first impression of Kinshasa, Zaire, was almost the same as my impression of India—hot, high humidity, and tropical. When I was teaching at Eakin School, I told my students about the hot, hot Belgian Congo (later changed to the country of Zaire), never dreaming that I would end up there. We were immediately taken to a guest hotel that served meals and housed families in individual cottages. We stayed at UMH (Union Missionary Hotel) for a few weeks while we made plans for the two older girls to remain in Kinshasa and attend the American School. They would have to board, and we arranged for Lisa to stay at the DCC Hostel (Disciples of Christ) and for Laura to live at MPH (Methodist Presbyterian Hostel). Both girls seemed very pleased and anxious for this new adventure, but I was not pleased and would miss them very much. I planned to teach Roger, Kate, and Nan their school-work, once again using the Calvert System.

From our first weeks in Kinshasa, I wrote my mother and her husband, Bob, these accounts:

October 8, 1969
Kinshasa

Dear Mother & Bob,

How good it was to have a letter waiting when we arrived! We left Bruxelles last Thursday Oct. 2nd and flew to Madrid, Spain. We stayed five days in Madrid and really enjoyed the Spanish sunshine. George and I went to a bullfight last Sunday and only stayed for an hour. It was too cruel a sport to really enjoy it! However the pageantry attached to the fight is interesting—the music, costumes, parade, etc. We saw two bulls killed and that was enough!

The highlight of our visit in Madrid was a day long excursion about 50 miles from Madrid to a town called Toledo. George and the children went one day while I stayed with Barbara at the hotel. It was so good that they insisted I take a day off and go to Toledo. It was a marvelous tour: a quaint medieval city with the old and new blended in perfect taste. We saw a cathedral probably the most beautiful in the world, surely more beautiful than the two big ones we've seen: Westminster Abbey (London) and Notre Dame in Paris.

Queen Isabella's crown was there and lots of other jewels, paintings, etc. One of the best spent days I've had this summer! I hope you received the picture that George and I sent to Windsor, North Carolina. It was made in a famous Spanish restaurant with our being serenaded by a group of strolling musicians.

We left Madrid yesterday, flew over Algiers, stopped in Nigeria for 2 hours and got into Kinshasa at about two o'clock this morning. We are staying in a mission hotel and George took the children off to the American school this morning. Africa reminds me so far of India with the tropical weather, palms, and high humidity.

I just wanted to let you know that we arrived safely and are here in Kinshasa. Let us hear from you soon and all the children send love and always enjoy your letters.

Bye for now and take care of yourselves.

Our love,

Barbara

October 16, 1969
Kinshasa

Dear Mother and Bob,

Greetings from hot, hot Africa! I can hardly believe that it's the middle of October because in this tropical climate we are only comfortable in sleeveless dress and sandals. We are comfortably situated for the time being in a guest hotel which is owned by all the various missions for their people passing through Kinshasa. The children are happily situated in the American school and Lisa & Laura won't go into Boarding school until we leave here. They have met other children that board and they are eager to move in now! In fact there was some question about a place for Laura and she was most unhappy that she might not get to stay here and board.

Lisa will be rooming with a girl whose mother was a friend of mine at Peabody. Isn't that a coincidence! I feel better about their staying here to board since I've seen the houses, met the couples that will take care of them, and visited the school. In fact Roger is begging to stay, but we feel he's too young! They have opportunities to swim, take piano and etc. Lisa is going to the American Ambassador's today to swim with her roommates. It will probably be the end of November before we are settled at our hospital. I'm sort of enjoying having three meals a day served to you, visiting with other wives, and no house responsibilities like cleaning etc. We have met so many lovely families and everyone spots our southern accent at once! We are gradually learning more and more French and it's surprising what the children can understand already.

I guess some things work out the way they are supposed to. For example the first night that we were in Africa, George saved a 2 yr. old European boy's life. He had swallowed something that stuck in his throat, and lived many miles away from Kinshasa. A Canadian doctor put the child on the plane and headed this way. En route the Canadian doctor had to do a partial tracheotomy, and when they arrived here, Dr. Bill Close, who is the personal doctor to the President of the Congo, called George to come see the child. They operated and so far the child is doing well. All send their love and write us real soon. I know you are glad to be home.

Love,

Barbara

October 21, 1969
Kinshasa

Dear Mother & Bob,

Hope this letter finds you back and settled in Franklin. I don't expect to be settled until sometime next month. Right now George has gone up to our hospital and will be checking any supplies needed so that we can bring them when we leave Kinshasa. I am comfortably settled in the Union Missionaire Hospitaliere guest house and enjoy meeting the other families coming and going plus having our meals served to us three times a day.

The children like the American school and are so excited because the astronauts are coming to Kinshasa tomorrow the 22nd and plans have been made for us to see them—maybe even shake their hand!

The shopping possibilities here in Kinshasa are unlimited, but things are so expensive. Twice what they are in the U.S. and Belgium. We got our car a week ago and are now working on getting the trunks through customs. You could never imagine the red tape that exists in Africa!

It's still very hot and the kids have enjoyed swimming. Every week the American Ambassador opens his pool to the American children and there is a pool at the house where Lisa will live.

Tell Edwyna and Gayle I need some more news from them and their families! Write soon and use this address until I let you know.

Our love,

Barbara

P.S. Did you get our picture from Spain?

On the day that we took Lisa to settle in at the DCC Hostel, I noticed a book on the table that belonged to the name Goodall. This quickly brought back memories of my Peabody College days when my good friend, Eunice Batey, was a student in my class. She later married Dr. Harry Goodall from Birmingham, Alabama, and went to Zaire, Africa, with the Disciples of Christ Mission. Previous to the year that we arrived in Africa, Eunice was killed in a small plane crash with the pilot and another friend. Her husband, Harry, later married the pilot's wife, Carol, and continued their medical work. The children of Eunice and Harry, Harry Jr., Julia, Page, and Lou Anne, were living in Kinshasa and studying at the American School. Our children became friends with the Goodall children, and it became very important to me to know Eunice's children. Julia became a doctor and returned to Kinshasa in the early 1990s to work in the American Clinic.

Our first duty in Africa was to spend two months in a rural mission situation before going up-country. This place was called Kimpese (African for cockroach), and the hospital was a cooperative effort of Presbyterians, American Baptists, Methodists, Mennonites, and the Congo Inland Mission.

We arrived late one afternoon with the four younger children, and I noticed that someone had drawn the first bath for us. I bathed one of the children, let the water go down the drain, and found out that the water drawn was our supply for the week! What to do? George and I picked up some buckets and walked down the dusty road to get some water from a neighbor's rain barrel. After that, we always had a rain barrel close by wherever we lived.

Our next-door neighbors in Kimpese were a British family, and the father was an anesthetist. One morning, his wife and I were talking while hanging out our wash. Out of the corner of my eye, I glimpsed some slow movement within the grass. Very calmly, I said, "That sure is a big snake." With that comment, we both jumped sky high and began to yell. "Serpent, serpent," we shouted, and some African workmen close by came to our aid. It was a big snake, some four or five feet long and very thick in diameter. It was called a Boom Slang, or tree snake, and always traveled in pairs. Needless to say, we did not sleep well that night. We knew that its mate was somewhere close.

The next day the mate was found caught up in some chicken wire next door. George and the anesthetist decided to clean up around the houses, and later, as I was busy inside, the small girl next door came into our house and casually mentioned that her daddy was just bitten by a snake. I went next door to inquire, only to find the father laid out on the couch, slowly turning blue, and George beginning to cut and suck out the venom. Fortunately, one of the nurses had run very quickly to the hospital and produced a serum to take care of its poison. George confirmed that the man was very close to death. I was beginning to think that life in Africa was all drama. How would I cope for two years?

After one month in Kimpese, George had to drive to Kinshasa to inquire about our household goods that were to arrive in Matadi, Zaire. This was a port city, and we were anxious to receive our barrels from home. A few days before we went to Kinshasa, a young man asked George if he could ride with us. We said yes, and the next day, he said that it would be his brother riding with us instead. On the day that we left, it was his goat that he brought for us to take to Kinshasa. We strapped the goat on top of the Volkswagen Combi and we listened to a sad cry from the goat every time the car went over a bump on the poorly paved road. I was learning that life in Africa was always full of surprises and unbelievable events.

My days were full of teaching Roger, Kate, and Nan, while Barbara played close by in the playpen. Before we left Brussels, I had bought a few Christmas gifts for the children, and we wrapped them in available comic paper for our first Christmas in Zaire. In sharing these simple pleasures of life, plus our great camping adventures, a bond of closeness was born within our family and would remain always. The following letters were written from Kimpese in November and December:

Nov. 26th
Kimpese

Dearest Mother & Bob,

"Happy Thanksgiving!" Even though it's hot as can be we will celebrate Thanksgiving tomorrow with turkey and the trimmings and houseguests too. Lisa and Laura are coming down late this afternoon with the other boarding children that live here and stay until Sunday. It is a three hour ride and George will take them back on Sunday afternoon! We are still halfway between Kinshasa (or Leopoldville) on the map and the seaport of Matadi. We will be here until Jan. 1st then go on to Boshwe where we'll be for 2 yrs. I never dreamed that I could make a home under such conditions of moving and etc. but we have and learned that good health and a happy family life are what count most. This is our third house since

June and we just move on in, clean up good, and use what's available!! I've had interesting neighbors and already enough interesting experiences to write a book! Someday between children and grandchildren I might do just that!

I finally had to give in and hire a houseboy because all the washing by hand, ironing, cooking out here, and other tasks just take too long. For example I have to boil and filter all of the drinking, toothbrush, and dishwashing water, all of the milk used has to be made up from powder, any desserts have to be baked, ice cream is made and we even make our own peanut butter. Antoine, the houseboy, washes and irons well so this leaves me free to cook and etc.

I want to give you Lisa & Laura's addresses:

Lisa Burrus
DCC Hostel
B.P. 4289
Kinshasa 2
Republique Du Congo

Laura Burrus
MPH Hostel
B.P. 4750
Kinshasa 2
Republique Du Congo

Lisa is in the Disciple of Christ (Woodmont Christian Church) hostel and Laura is in the Methodist-Presby. hostel. Write soon.

Our love,

Barbara

Dec. 14, 1969
Kimpese

Dearest Mother & Bob,

The main purpose of this letter is to wish you both a very "Merry Christmas" and a new year filled with health and happiness!! Everyone is fine and looking for Santa Claus here in Africa! George has returned from his trip to the Congo Estuary with the secretary of World Health for Congo. They vaccinated the people and held clinics along the river. We are looking for Lisa and Laura this Friday, the 19th. They will be here until Jan. 5th at which time we will all leave Kimpese and go back to Kinshasa for a week or so before going up the river to the hospital where George will serve. They are supposed to be building us a house and I only hope it will be finished so that I can get settled for a while! When I think of all the traveling we have done in 1969 starting with the San Francisco medical meeting and on to Africa with Europe in between, it makes me right dizzy! However, I'm sure in my old age I will have lots of memories! Ha! At least life is never dull! Ha!

Barbara is now one of the "gang" if you can believe it! She plays, scraps, and screams for her share and believe me they pay attention! She walks well and tries to talk some. She is a real blonde with blue eyes and still looks like her daddy!

Let me know about the wedding and be sure to give our love to Grannie. I would like to read the paper account if it's available to send.

Give our love to all on Christmas Eve and think on the fact that we're together as a family and healthy, and that we'll return for sure in two years.

All our love,

Barbara

Dec. 26, 1969
Kimpese

Dear Mother & Bob,

We have more going on here than a three-ring circus! Besides the six energetic children I have one energetic husband, and two houseboys: one that speaks no English, only French and Portuguese and the other speaks very little English, French and Kicongo! All day people come to the front and back doors selling vegetables, fruit, and ivory items plus baskets etc. and also we have many beggars and etc. at the door! Believe it or not I made it through Christmas and want to report a happy and joyous one with our family. Everyone seemed to enjoy and appreciate what old Santa bought! Nan and Barbara got dolls (I bought them in Belgium), Roger got a big front light for his bicycle which was part of Christmas, but he and Kate got the bikes in November and we decided not to hide them, but let them go on and enjoy riding them. Kate got some Barbie clothes, a nurse outfit, pajamas, books, puzzles, all the girls got pajamas, and slips that I had bought in Belgium! Each stocking had a big candy bar, bubble gum, a pack of Chiclets, 1 apple, some pencils, 1 pen, some pretty hair ribbons (except my son!) and 1 Zaire ($2.00). I had been saving the stuff for 3 or 4 months. Kate and Roger enjoyed a school Christmas party to which Nan was invited and all of the five big ones were in the Christmas play. Kate was an angel and Roger was a shepherd. Nan, Laura, & Lisa were in the choir. We had baked ham for Christmas dinner since a turkey was not available like we had for Thanksgiving. The girls and I have done lots of baking during Christmas and George says my chocolate cake and icing are the best in the world. All on a gas stove too! (No mixes!) When you have to do or make something or else do without it's surprising how you quickly manage it! We have enjoyed our two months here and have enjoyed the 100 friends from Canada, England, Belgium & America that are here at this hospital. However, we leave the 2nd of January and will be in Kinshasa for about 2 weeks before our trip up the river to Boshwe, our home for the next 2 years. We'll stay at UMH so keep this same address until I write a new one! All the family are well and send their love. I've watched 3 operations lately and enjoy going on the wards to observe George's work.

Our love,

Barbara

After our stay in Kimpese, we went back to Kinshasa, said good-bye to the big girls, and prepared to go up-country, or to the jungle. I had some reservations about the small plane that would carry us to Boshwe (this name was later changed to Bosobe). However, in order to be brave in front of my four children, I climbed into the six seater and prayed for a safe journey into the unknown. We had left our Volkswagen Combi in Kinshasa because the roads up-country were too bad for cars, except jeeps or trucks.

We landed about three or four hours later in a small Swedish mission called Semendua. This was the center of Swedish Baptist work in the area, and some nine or ten Swedish families welcomed us for the night. We would stay here for the night, then go by jeep the next day to Boshwe. Boshwe had no airstrip, so this was our only way to reach our mission station. Little did I know the part that Semendua would play in our lives in the years ahead. The Swedes made us feel very welcome, and after a covered-dish meal of Swedish food and a good night's rest, we prepared to go to Boshwe.

Jan. 19, 1970
Boshwe

Dearest Mother & Bob,

This letter will not be too long because it has to leave Boshwe this afternoon in order to be mailed for the week. Mail will not post as quickly as it did in Bruxelles or in Kinshasa, but keep writing as I will! It was a thrill to talk to you, Bob, Gayle, and Mama B. on Thurs.

Jan. 8th! Thank Jack Schmidt again the next time you see him or talk to him! We'll try to do it as often as possible when we're in Kinshasa!

Well we left Kinshasa last Tues. the 13th of Jan. after an exhausting week of buying supplies & food for 6 mo. Of course we'll be in and out of Kinshasa for the next 2 years, but thought we'd start off with a good supply. The plane trip was very interesting with a good view of African jungles, rivers, plains, and villages! We went within about 120 kilometers of our station & by jeep over some very bumpy roads the rest of the way! However, we found a warm welcome from the Swedish people and Africans as well. A nice house awaited us and after traveling and living from suitcases & trying to recall "where I put what" for about 8 mo. it was good to find a home! However, they are building us a nice house just in sight of this one and in about 3 mo. I have to move again. But this time we can all pick up belongings and walk over to the new house. I have already unpacked those 16 trunks and 3 barrels and won't touch them again until we pack up to come home! We have four helpers: a cook, nurse, gardener, and laundry man. They all speak a tribal language and just as I was learning to converse in French, they don't understand much of it! Tell Bob he should see my goat I received as a gift today from the chief of the village. He really gave it to George who in turn gave it to me! (Ha!)

All of the children are fine, and I started school for Roger and Kate yesterday. Be sure to write to Lisa and Laura often. We had three good weeks with them over Christmas and they will be home in March for Easter and in June for the summer! The palm trees here in Boshwe are beautiful and we have orchids and gardenias also!

Better close and finish a letter for the girls before the truck leaves. There are only two more families here (they are Swedish), but the younger one (33) is so attractive and speaks English. We have already had some good fellowship. Tell Bob I miss your good cooking, but can't complain about the antelope we had for lunch. Write!

Our love,

Barbara

March 19, 1970
Boshwe

Dearest Mother & Bob,

Mail is so slow that I'm not sure how often you hear, but I keep writing!

Things are going fairly well here with only the usual daily ups and downs. Right now the electricity is broken and we have no lights! We usually only have electricity from 7 p.m. to 9 p.m., so I really don't miss it. We use kerosene lamps.

George and Nan went to Kinshasa last Sunday to buy some insulin for the hospital and will return tomorrow. It's really lonesome without them, however, Roger has had an eleven-year-old Swedish boy here for a week and the two of them are enough to keep one busy and occupied. They both eat everything in sight and when the grocery is seven hours away, supplies are more precious!

The girls will be home in less than a week for an Easter vacation of about ten days. Laura's hostel parents and their 16-year-old son are flying up with Lisa and Laura, so for ten days I will have lots of company. This means 11 people to feed 3 times a day, but this isn't too important if I have my family together.

Roger thinks the men and boys will go hunting for a leopard, so he's very excited. He will be ten years old this Sunday, and Kate will be nine next Friday! Africa is an exciting place for a ten-year-old boy, much more interesting than his school books!

Barbara, Nan, and Kate are fine! Kate & Nan have bicycles (Nan's has training wheels!) and Barbara sits on the tricycle that she has inherited from Nan!

I hope this letter finds you, Bob, Grannie, and "Miss D" well and maybe enjoying some of spring. I missed a touch of winter, and will miss spring since I like it best of all. I would like a report on the house at 2103 Golf Club so maybe you could stop and check the next time you pass.

All our love,

Barbara & family

April 8, 1970
Boshwe

Dearest Mother & Bob,

Even though there seems to be a mail strike in the U.S., we have received several letters lately in good time from you. It is always so good to hear from home! We had a very good Easter and, of course, Lisa & Laura being here made the difference! They flew in on Thurs., March the 26th. When I say "they," I mean Lisa, Mr. & Mrs. Red Alger, and their 16-year-old son, John. Laura had come the week before with her daddy and Nan from Kinshasa, so she had a longer vacation! We are about five hours from an airstrip, so George, Roger, Kate, Nan, and Laura took the jeep and met them. Mr. & Mrs. Alger are Laura's hostel parents and are from West Virginia. On Sat. morning after they arrived, George, Roger, Red Alger, and John Alger loaded up the jeep with enough food and water for four days and went on a safari further into the jungle. They came back with a small civet (type of cat) and plenty of wild tales! What adventures for a ten-year-old boy! Their plane left the Kemper airstrip on Thurs. April 2nd and George insisted we all take them to the plane, so we loaded up in the jeep and took the 5 hr. trip over terrible roads to see them off and then we had the 5 hr. trip home (all the same day)! It has taken me since then to feel rested again because the heat here saps everyone's energy! I enjoyed the girls so much and we talked and talked. Lisa did some sewing and plans to do more this summer. I also enjoyed Pat Alger to chat with since the three ladies here at Boshwe are Swedish and very nice, but not much company. Two speak good English, are young and attractive, but I guess the cultural backgrounds make a difference. I really enjoy the older woman better, but I have to speak French with her and this limits our conversations (because of my poor French, not hers)! Roger, Kate, Lisa & Laura speak good French, some Lingala (the African language), and Kate speaks some Swedish! Nan knows some French and Swedish, and Barbara only concentrates on English and the main word is No! You know how two-year-olds only say no to everything!

Better close and get this ready for anyone passing in the direction of civilization. Write soon and take care of yourselves! I miss you both.

Love,

Barbara

Wednesday
May 6, 1970
Boshwe

Dearest Mother and Bob,

I hope this letter finds Grannie Judd better and perhaps out of the hospital by now. We haven't received John's letter yet that you mentioned he was writing. I guess Spring has arrived and how I miss my pretty yard. When I get home I hope I never have to leave it again except when they carry me out! (Ha!) Of course hot weather continues here as all the year round, but some days are better than others!! I always welcome rain!

We talked to Laura on the short wave phone Monday, and she and Lisa were fine. Laura asked permission to bring home a cat and Lisa wanted to buy a new swim suit. George said "Yes" to both requests. They will be home in about five weeks for the summer!

Roger and Kate are in their last month of school, and I hope learning something! Roger has just finished studying the Congo Valley, Netherlands, and Switzerland in Geography and it has been so much more interesting for him since he has been to all three places.

We have been enjoying fresh grapefruit and oranges from the trees in our yard. These are good sources of vitamin C for the children. Barbara is at that very difficult age of 20 mo. when they climb out of bed all the time, and everything is either "me" or "no"! Her favorite words besides these are "Nan" and "Ka-Ka" (Kate).

Nan is counting the days until May 17th, and she will be five years old! She, Kate, & Roger are planning a party and have made favors and decorations, and invitations.

I wish you could hear the children speak French. They have also learned some Swedish and Lingala (the native language).

Guess this is all for now. Write soon and give our love to Edwyna & Gayle's families.

Our love,

Barbara

The village in which we would work was inhabited by the Basakata tribe. The Basakata people lived mostly between the two navigable rivers, Kasai and Lukenie, and spoke Lingala. French is the official language of Zaire, but some of the people spoke Kisakata, their mother tongue. The area is rural, and the people live in small villages. They cultivate their main crop, cassava, a tubular plant in the forest, and other crops are rice, corn, coffee, peanuts, and some potatoes. Local traders took coffee and cassava to sell in Kinshasa by van or boat, and in turn would bring back sugar, soap, salt, buckets, pots, hoes, shoes, clothes, notebooks, and pens to sell to the people. We ate some native dishes; however, cassava was not tasty at all!

The Basakata people have a matriarchal society, and thus, you see the women carrying heavy loads of wood, water on their heads, and babies on their backs. They work much harder than the men at every task.

Mere words will never describe the welcome that awaited us in Boshwe. Our family stood on a small balcony on the second floor of the

This sight always amazed us.

school while children by the hundreds marched and danced to drums in true African style. Each time they rotated around the school, the rhythm, dance, and drums became more and more intense. My children were wide-eyed and quite surprised at the events. They presented us with a chicken, eggs, and peanuts—symbols of thanks, welcome, and good fortune. It had been several years since a doctor had been in Boshwe, and the future looked much brighter for them.

We were given a small adequate cottage with four small bedrooms, a living and dining room combination, and kitchen separate from the house. We used one of the bedrooms for a schoolroom for Roger, Kate, and Nan.

The Swedes had arranged for a cook named Moise, a nanny for Barbara named Esther, a gardener named Iyuli, and a washerman named Oscar. I spent my days organizing the household, trying out my French, and meeting my new neighbors. Two Swedish families lived in Boshwe, Anna Britta and Torre Carlson and Brigette and Hokan Westergen. Anna Britta and Brigette were nurses, and Torre and Hokan were heads of the business office and construction for the hospital.

Before coming up-country, we had purchased flour, sugar, dried milk, and canned goods for our meals. We used as much of the local fruit and vegetables that were available, plus fish and some beef brought by a Catholic priest from time to time.

Our house in Bosobe (Boshwe). Little did I know how much time would be spent here!

We ate our first meal in Boshwe at Anna Britta's house, and her cook was named Jacob. Little did I know that some twenty years later, I would depend upon Jacob to cook for George and me. However, I am getting ahead of my story, so back to 1970. Many times while riding my bike back from the hospital, I would pass Iyuli, the gardener, leading a goat by a string. I did not think much about it until a month later when some teachers came to ask George if they could use the extra room in the school for a visiting professor. When asked why we were the ones to give permission, it seems that the doctor's goat occupied that room all the time. I had forgotten that the goat had been a gift from the chief upon our arrival!

For about a month, Moise, the cook, had tried to explain a situation to me concerning washing the clothes. It had something to do with Oscar, the washer, but I could not understand. Finally, after taking me out behind the kitchen and pointing to the big black kettle where the clothes were being boiled and washed in hot water, I got the picture. Each day after the washing was done, Oscar failed to empty the water for clean water the next day. Therefore, our clothes were being washed in the same dirty water as the preceding day. The next morning I dismissed Oscar, got out the metal scrub board, and experienced my great-grandmother's mode of washing. The hot sun did add to my labor. Later, I gave Oscar another chance, but some changes were made.

The days passed and George worked on as best he could with limited resources. One day the chief of the region came for a visit, and I offered him tea and cookies. As I passed the plate of cookies, he took the plate and cookies to take home. I made a mental note to give him some cookies next time on a napkin!

For some time, it had bothered George that there was no airstrip in Boshwe, and it was a day's journey to Semendua and the airstrip. He had discussed with the Swedes the convenience of a plane bringing medicine into Boshwe; however, they enjoyed the day's trip to visit their fellow countrymen in Semendua. While he was having tea and cookies with the chief, George mentioned the value of an airstrip to the surrounding region. The chief responded by saying that he would supply the manpower to cut out an airstrip.

That was on a Friday afternoon, and on Monday morning, five hundred men, women with hoes and babies on their backs, and young folks came to work. The Swedes could not believe it and were very surprised at the response. After one month of intense labor, mostly by the women, the airstrip took shape. The German government had given an ambulance for the hospital's work, and George hitched a large log to the back of the vehicle. Each day, the family rode the airstrip several times to smooth the surface of the airstrip. The surface was packed with "matuka," which is an ant-hill material that has been pulverized and made firm. The children thought that it was great fun to have an outing on the airstrip.

We were unsure about the landing surface for a large plane until one day we heard a great buzz in the sky. The whole village ran down to the airstrip where a plane had landed. The pilot stepped out of the plane and asked, "Where am I? This is not on my map!" He was lost and almost out of gas. We explained our location, and he left the area. The Swedes later said that we planned this event, but it was a surprise for us also. It did prove that at last Boshwe had an airstrip. As George and I used it for many years to come and go with medicine and supplies, we felt that it was one of our better gifts to the people for their health.

The two big girls, Lisa and Laura, came up for their Easter vacation, and it was so good to have my family all together again. Pat and Red Alger, Laura's hostel parents, came with them. We enjoyed a weekend of games and conversation, and the men did some hunting. Laura came home with a small cat in a cage, and because I felt guilty about her being away at such an early age, she was allowed to keep it. I have never liked cats, so it was a real concession for me. One night, our group slipped out into the jungle and hid behind a large bush. We watched in awe as the natives danced around the fire to the beat of huge drums. Many nights, we sat in our bungalow and heard drums, singing, and chanting in the distance.

As the work continued, George felt that maybe we had come too soon to the region. The Swedes were more intent upon building the plant than concentrating on medical problems. At about that time, Dr. William Close again contacted George to come to Kinshasa and work with about thirty other medical specialists that were coming to Kinshasa to form FOMECO. Since the work at Boshwe was progressing slowly, George accepted the offer, which meant that we would be moving to Kinshasa. That was good news for me, because I had taught Roger his fourth-grade work, Kate the third grade, and Nan some kindergarten, and now all five would be able to go to the American School and be at home as a family. Barbara was only two years old at the time.

The following year, 1970–1971, was a most pleasant one in many respects. About fifteen other American families came to Kinshasa to work with FOMECO, and I welcomed the end of some isolation in the jungle. Our family was housed in one side of a very large duplex, and in the other side was a wonderful family of six from Kansas. They were Mary (Winkie) and Dr. Roger Youmans and their four children, Grace, Joy, John, and young Roger. Grace was Laura's age, Joy was Roger's age and a great friend of Katie's, John was seven, and young Roger and Nan were kindergarten age.

Our house had once been the German Embassy, and a high wall and gate made us feel secure. Winkie had a lovely trained voice and had brought her piano to Africa. Every morning after the FOMECO school bus picked up the nine children from our houses alone, I enjoyed hearing her play and practice or having a second cup of coffee with her. George and Roger Youmans were kindred spirits in their desire to serve in a medical capacity to an underdeveloped country. Roger and Winkie had been to Zaire before the 1967 small revolution and continued to serve in FOMECO for ten years. They returned in the 1990s to work in Ghana. Sometime in the 1980s, their son, John, was killed in an automobile accident, and in 1994, my good friend, Winkie, died of cancer. Shortly after her death, Roger Youmans sent me a gold charm in the shape of Africa. Winkie had asked for me to receive it after her death. It was made by a young African whom she had led to the Lord.

When we came to Kinshasa from the bush, we brought Esther, a young girl of sixteen, with us, since she had been Barbara's nanny for a year. We also had a cook and houseboy who did some of the food shopping in the large outdoor market in Kinshasa. His name was Phillip, from Angola, and he could do quite well with my recipes. At first he secured cassava or dried fish for Esther, but I encouraged her to eat with us and to try "our food." It was Esther's pronunciation of Barbara's name that gave her the nickname of "Bozi."

FOMECO built small prefabricated houses for their staff, and it became quite an attractive subdivision near the city. All of the specialists worked in the Mama Yemo Hospital, named after Mobutu's mother. We especially enjoyed the company of Dr. and Mrs. Cal Johnson and Dr. and Mrs. Amin Jazab. George first knew Dr. Jazab in Nashville years ago when he trained at St. Thomas Hospital. They were the parents of two girls, Elham and Aram, who were friends of Lisa and Laura. Years later, Aram settled in Nashville, and we continued our friendship with Amin and Neshat when they would come to visit her.

We knew Inga and Cal Johnson in Kimpese, and before moving to their FOMECO home, they lived with us in Kinshasa for one month prior to the house being finished. They had four small sons and occupied one of our bedrooms for the month. Inga was very creative and helped me in the household activities and food preparation. I have a hard time now imagining the eight of our family, plus Esther, and the six of their family living in harmony, but somehow you make do and adjust in foreign situations better than in your own environment. The following letter was written very soon after we had moved to Kinshasa:

Sept. 9, 1970
Kinshasa

Dearest Mother & Bob,

I have received your letter telling about your holiday, but decided to send this letter on to Windsor, North Carolina, anyway. I know that I have been a very poor writer this summer, but my time has not been my own! The last letter I wrote was from a vacation in Boende that was supposed to be for one week. President Mobutu's private plane came for us a week earlier than planned. Lisa stayed with the Goodalls for another week. We dropped George, Laura and Nan off in Boshwe to pack up those sixteen trunks and three barrels, and Kate, Barbara and I came on to Kinshasa. I forgot that I had told friends they could use the house while passing through Kinshasa and when I got home there were six folks living here, Laura's last year hostel parents, their two kids, and a young couple just arrived for this new medical program. They stayed almost 2 wks, then George, Laura & Nan flew back with our trunks (still not completely unpacked). Lisa & Roger arrived, then when it seemed to be only our family, other friends coming to Kinshasa to live had to stay with us since their house wasn't finished. They had 4 small boys, 1 dog, 1 parrot! I was feeding 12–15 folks three times a day for three weeks and believe me it's a sure way to diet! I lost 8 lbs. bringing me to a total of 22 lbs. lost in Africa. About 25 American doctors are coming to open this new hospital sponsored by President Mobutu.

Finally school started and Lisa is a freshman, Laura a seventh grader, Roger in the fifth, Kate in the fourth, and Nan in Kindergarten. All five are taking French lessons and speak good French. Baba sent me the picture of Edwyna in the paper and I enjoyed the writeup. Also the whole family enjoyed Bob's picture at the market.

Barbara had her second birthday last week and she is something else in determination! She makes me feel 40 yrs. a year before I'm due to be 40. She's had stitches three times this summer because of falls and climbing. I would appreciate your taking care of a wedding present for Susan. Use your judgment and get the money from Catherine. Give my best to Grannie, and take care of yourselves. We miss you.

Our love,

Barbara

Our days were full of school activities, swimming at the American Club or Embassy, joining in the many services and projects of the International Church, and discovering the many mysteries of Kinshasa. I sometimes thought that Kinshasa was then at its height in European products and borrowed culture. The Belgian people made it an interesting city in which to live and function. We still had our Volkswagen Combi, which I drove around the city, and FOMECO furnished George with a Mazda for his transportation. Believe it or not, our best restaurant in the world was right there in Kinshasa. It was named La Deveniér, and we treated some of Lisa's and Laura's friends on Lisa's fourteenth birthday. The French cooking was simply superb, plus the French know how to serve an elegant meal.

We enjoyed some hospitality in Dr. Close's home, but we never met his daughter, Glenn. At the time, she was in Europe singing with the group Up with People. We did attend her sister's wedding reception that spring of 1971, and I spent the better part of the day practicing what to say in French when introduced to President Mobutu. However, it was all in vain, since he never came to the reception.

I mentioned earlier that we lived in a rather secure compound with a large stone wall and gate. We also shared an evening guard with the Youmans family. However, one morning I asked George where his Mazda was, and he answered, "Just outside the front door as always." "Well," I said, "The car has simply vanished!" The guard said that he had been taking a bath on the back property and did not understand how the theft could happen. Roger's clarinet was in the car, and months later, we found out that it had been used as a taxi in Kinshasa, adding many miles to the car. There were many white Mazdas in Kinshasa, since FOMECO furnished the doctors with such a car.

Dr. Close asked George to accompany President Mobutu on some of his trips by boat up-country to relieve some of these trips away from Mrs. Close and family. Once George and the president were playing a game of chess on board. While George struggled to speak French, General Mobutu said if possible he would rather speak English. George felt relieved at best. The president was kind enough to loan us the use of one of his DC-3s for two vacations. Once we went farther north up to Boende to visit the Goodall family, and there in that jungle retreat, I experienced my first fondue dinner by candlelight.

The next trip was one that our family will always remember as the best. We flew up to Parc Albert for a sightseeing safari of African animals. On the way up, we flew over an active volcano that was known by the pilot. He banked the plane, and the children ran to one side and viewed the red lava flowing from the center. Then he flew around and banked on the other side for similar sights. What a geography lesson for our children! Also, we viewed lots of hippos bathing in the Rwindi River. The Parc was near the Uganda border, and we flew to Goma.

Parc Albert (now called Parc Mobutu) was a retreat for guests who were interested in viewing the African animals in their native habitat. Each guest was given a thatched-roof cottage for the duration of the stay. They told us that we were given the cottage used by Queen Fabiola and King Baudouin I of Belgium a few years ago. It was furnished nice enough for that to be true! Guests ate in a large dining room in a main building. Roger had taken a school friend with us, Michael Weaver from California. His father worked with FOMECO.

The next day after arriving at the Parc, we were given a driver and a Volkswagen Combi with a top that opened up for us to stand and view

Our family across the "imaginary line" of the equator.

the animals. We saw sights firsthand that many only see in the *National Geographic* or the movies. We watched a pride of lions stalk and devour a buffalo, elephants walking in a straight line toward the river, hippos in the water, hyenas, leopards, wildebeest, giraffes, and gazelles leaping along. It was so much better than a zoo.

George heard that we were only a day's trip away from Pygmy country, so he hired a car and driver for our journey. On the way, the driver stopped the car and said we had just passed the equator. Since the equator is an imaginary line, we all lined up across the road for a picture. We arrived late that afternoon in Benie, Zaire, and were unable to find accommodations for two nights. However, we braved one night in the Benie Motel and set out the next day to see the Pygmies, plus find a room for that night.

George wanted to go into an authentic Pygmy village, so we walked single file into the vast Ituri forest and came upon such a village. All the way into the forest, I could hear sounds behind the trees and felt that we were watched while we entered their territory. They received us in a frenzy, as they ran about grabbing other leaves to add to their basic ones. They were small people with very large stomachs and short legs and arms. They danced around the fire for us, and our children joined them in the dance. George treated several for conjunctivitis, and the chief gave us some poisonous darts as a gift. It is said that the Pygmies live nearer to earth and nature than any other ethnic group.

A missionary family close by offered us a room for the night, and we enjoyed their hospitality for dinner and rest. They were keeping some Pygmy twins for a few months, and I fed a bottle to one of them. She was very, very small and fit in my hand. After we returned to Parc Albert, the president's plane awaited us, and we left for Kinshasa.

For me, the highlight of my year in Kinshasa was a two-week trip up the Congo River aboard a hospital boat built by President Mobutu for aiding his people's health. These journeys were to examine the population for illness, and each day we docked at a village on the water. Clinics were held, people were treated, and if necessary brought aboard for an operation. The boat was well equipped with an operating room and two wards, one for men and one for women. If people needed an operation, they stayed with us until the boat came back by their village. In a few cases, we took them back to Kinshasa for long-term treatment. We had left the six children with Esther and two English ladies who worked in Dr. Close's clinic. The only complaint from the children when we returned home was that they were tired of roast beef, Yorkshire pudding, and trifle for dessert!

Our accommodations on the boat were very pleasant, and we enjoyed the company of several other couples from FOMECO. The meals were prepared and served to us, and the day was mine to explore the boat, read, and view the activity along the riverbanks. Many people gathered at the docks with their cassava and other food to be taken by other boats to Kinshasa. We went up the river as far as Inongo, a beautiful beach with lovely palm trees.

I kept a ten-day journal of my trip up the Congo River, and the following words convey my observations and thoughts:

Friday
March 12, 1971

Dear Poppi,
Dearest Mother and Bob,

Well, this letter will be quite different from the rest because it will take me ten days to write it. The reason for this is because I am writing a diary of my ten-day voyage up the Congo River aboard the "Marie Antoinette" hospital boat. It was named after Madame Mobutu, and it's the most modern and well equipped hospital boat you could imagine! For ten days, we will sail up the huge Congo River north to the area called Bandundu (check your map!) and stop at villages, examine the sick, bring the real sick ones back to the boat, operate, and etc. The first voyage, over 1,000 people were seen and treated. About 30 persons are aboard, including an American nurse and a young doctor and his wife from Canada! I was brought along for two reasons: one for a needed break from routine and the other to assist George. He says I'll be in the operating room before the trip is over—I'll let you know day by day!!!!

The children are all fine and in good hands! Two widowed friends, one a lab technician (American) and the other a receptionist at the clinic (English), will stay at the house the ten days and friends and other doctors will check each day.

We sailed about noon today, a beautiful sunny warm day. Our rooms are very nice, bedroom, bath, and sitting room (even with piped in music!). Of course, the view of the jungle along the river bank is outstanding with the palms and we've seen dug-out boats along the way with Africans fishing. This boat was a dream of the president's and Dr. Close and no expense has been spared to give the Congolese people up the river good medical care. The dining room is like any big cruise ship. For lunch we had filet, soup, french fries, coffee, and crepes.

Tonight we enjoyed sitting on deck and watching a full moon on the water.

Saturday, March 13th

If the rest of the days are as dramatic and full as today has been, I'm not sure I can last out the trip! We stopped at the first large village up the river and weeded out the really sick ones from the ones that only wanted to see the inside of the boat. George had said all along that I was going along to work and assist him in operations. I said, "Sure," never dreaming he was serious, however, now I know! At 3:00 p.m. we scrubbed, gowned, masked, and entered the O.R. Edwyna would have loved to see me passing instruments!! I had trouble remembering how to pass scissors and of course George would yell (to the delight of the Congolese nurses). Finally I told them I definitely was not afraid of him. He said that Cooley and DeBakey would have fired me on the spot! (That's what I wanted him to do so that I could take a sun bath on the deck!) The case, by the way, was a huge hernia and took three hours to do! George had to leave for an emergency just as he was closing it up so I first assisted a young Congolese doctor sew the man up! By the way, I have Polaroid pictures to verify my operating room assistance! After the operation was over, George seriously said he was sure I would faint and was very surprised that I didn't. I never entertained the thought!! However, I was quite tired at the end of the day and was amazed at what the operating room drama does to your energy! We sailed off about midnight, further on up the river.

Sunday, March 14th

This morning was spent helping George do a hernia operation. Several other cases were being done so I was the only one to help plus a circulating nurse. It's amazing to me how one knows when and what to cut even after years of study and practice.

I failed to mention that a Catholic Nun who is a nurse at the Kinshasa General Hospital is along on the trip and has the best sense of humor you could imagine! She speaks the language of the people and this is a joy to see her communicate with them.

The afternoon was a page out of most geography books! We took the 18 ft. inboard-outboard boat, made by "Glaston" of Austin, Texas, and went up close to tiny villages that were unable to get to the boat. Everyone wanted some of the pills and if they weren't already hurting, they suddenly had pain. Here again they had to weed out the really sick ones. Here we saw the small thatched huts, primitive living by the water's edge and people eager for attention and help. They could not pay, but insisted on giving us eggs as we left. Earlier a chief had come aboard in his orange robes and presented a chicken to one of the white nurses. He liked having his picture made! A Swiss family came aboard for dinner tonight and after a visit we carried them back to their home by the 18 ft. boat. I can tell my grand-children about a beautiful moonlight ride on the Congo River someday!

Monday, March 15th

George went out about 4:30 a.m. to hunt buffalos, and I spent the morning rolling bandages for the operating room. The day ended in a bad storm and rainfall and the boat rocked quite a bit. Age has cured me of seasickness evidently!

Tuesday, March 16th

Today we stopped at a very large village, and in the course of the day, 250 persons were seen. This does not mean 250 sick ones, but most of them needed vitamins and malaria medicine. Several were admitted for surgery, pneumonia, tropical ulcers, and some very sick babies were retained. This morning I helped George in surgery, and this afternoon I helped on the ward taking temp. etc.

I wish now that I had spent my four years in nursing! About five o'clock this afternoon we left the boat to visit the local hospital and Catholic mission. The boat works in cooperation with any hospitals along the way and will carry some patients back to Kinshasa for orthopedic treatment, etc. About 5,000 people gathered along the banks tonight for movies shown by the boat!

Wednesday, March 17th

Today began in surgery! The boat has two O.R. rooms, x-ray room, four consultation rooms, eight examining rooms, sterilizing room, physiotherapy room, pharmacy, women's ward, men's ward, gym room, office—all of this is on the medical floor (2nd floor). The first floor is for laundry (giant washers and dryers), kitchens (2), crew's quarters, and etc. The third floor is living quarters for the staff (2 suites like ours and other rooms, lounge, and dining areas). Fourth floor is the radio room, captain's quarters, and chart and steering areas. The day ended with some folk music while the Canadian doctor played his guitar. Look at your map and find Bandundu! We spent the night here and will work here tomorrow. It has 40,000 persons so the work here will be in cooperation with the Congolese hospital here! Notice how close we're getting to Boshwe. We might go there for a day. I'm anxious to get off the boat in the morning and explore the shops. Lots of nice cloth and you never know what you will find!

Thursday, March 18th

It is getting close to Roger's birthday and I hope we are back by Monday. Mama has had her rest and anxious now to see my "gang." I left the boat today for a walk into the town of Bandundu and a look at the stores. I bought some Congolese cloth and some small gifts for the children. By American standards the stores away from Kinshasa are not much, but interesting to explore. I found some TABU body powder in one store today! Can you imagine going up the Congo River and freezing?? Well believe it or not the air conditioners on the boat make it necessary to keep a sweater handy at all times! Sounds peculiar??

Friday, March 19th

I believe that keeping house and tending to children is easier than the operating room for me! I spent the morning assisting George and for 3 hrs. I had to stand and help. I am learning the instruments and how to pass them, but inside everything still looks the same to me! I enjoy seeing the Congolese babies on board with their mamas. If the mama is sick and becomes a patient, then the baby has to come on board too because of nursing. Sometimes the 2 or 3 yr. old is the sick one and mama comes with it and also brings a baby along that's nursing.

George is getting lots of good pictures as we travel and the scenery is fantastic at some spots. Tomorrow we go to Kutu (on map) and on to Loch Leopold II, a beautiful lake.

Saturday, March 20th

After Kutu we moved on to our last stop north to a village called Inongo, probably the most picturesque village we've seen on the trip. The afternoon was spent in operating, a three hour one and a bloody one! It's hard to stand there for so long and I'm tired when we finish. George says I would never make it doing five hearts a day! (Who wants to!!) We ran out of some important drugs a few days ago and we radioed to Kinshasa to send some up. Yesterday a helicopter arrived, landed on the helicopter pad on the boat and brought us the needed drugs. Last night the chief of this territory had a dinner for the four doctors aboard. I chose to stay on the boat and eat food that I knew was good!! There was a tremendous wind during the night and the waves were very high and the boat rocked all night!

Sunday, March 21st

A morning of surgery! We were doing a case on one man, and when we inquired how he was doing (he had a spinal, so he was awake) he said, "Fine, take your time—I'm enjoying this!" It was probably more attention than he had had in a lifetime!

The afternoon was free after 4:00 p.m. so George and I took a long walk down the white sandy beach and enjoyed a beautiful sunset on the water. You could almost feel that you were in Hawaii with the tall palm trees, white sandy beach, and water lapping on the sand, but near all of this is the poorly nourished child or some such other scene and you are suddenly back in Africa! We will leave Inongo in the morning and head back to Kinshasa. We will pick up really sick patients on the return trip to carry back to Kinshasa General Hospital.

This whole trip has been something to remember for a long time; good impressions, bad impressions, gratitude for good medical care, suffering and relief etc. Now it's time to head back to my children and become involved in the work I know best—tending to them!!

Give our love to all, and it's with a thankful heart that I say, see you soon! George plans to leave here somewhere around the 20th. I told him not to tell all about Africa, leave some tales for me!

Our love,

Barbara

By that time, it was the spring of 1971, and plans were in our minds for our return to Nashville. However, George was interested in a meeting to be held in the States, so he took Nan with him and returned to America. The other children were finishing up their school year, so Nan was chosen to go.

The following letter was written to George in the States during that spring trip:

Kinshasa

Dearest Daddy & Nan,

Oh, how we miss both of you! Everyday Barbara says, "Where's my daddy? Where's Nan?" If you ask her where you are, she says, "In an airplane"! Things are about the same here! Bruce Wolf is still in bed and they are talking about operating. Lisa practices sometimes twice a day and seems to enjoy it! Roger was the soloist last Friday night and he really sang out!! He had a swimming birthday party last Saturday and it was something to keep an eye on those seven boys in the pool. Today I will take Kate, Joy, and Jennifer Birch swimming for Kate's birthday! Laura misses the Youman's (they moved last Saturday) and she and Grace think up (or try to) a school excuse everyday to visit! Roger flew up to Gemana on Monday to see Mobutu's mother, but said it was a useless trip (whatever that means!) Ever since the Youmans have moved Desireé has talked about thieves. I told him if he let just one more thief into the yard I would find another sentinel.

If you find that you'll be home any earlier, cable me!! We are all excited about Poppi's coming back with you and hope you found things fine there. Be sure to put some flowers on Ellen's grave and let me know how my tree is!! You and Nan must remember every detail of the visit because we are eager for news. We received your card from Greece! We love you both so much—hurry home to us!

Our love,

Mama, Lisa, Laura, Roger, Kate, Barbara

On the way home, Nan and George went by way of Israel and took a two-day sightseeing tour of the Holy Lands. We have a picture of tired little Nan standing by the Wailing Wall in Jerusalem. Unbeknownst to us, it was just before she broke out with mumps!

During George's absence, Laura had a bad case of pneumonia, but Dr. Roger Youmans took excellent care of her at home. We had been blessed with good health during our stay in Africa. Lisa had the lead in the school play, and we enjoyed end-of-school activities.

After about three weeks at home, George and Nan returned by way of Lambarene, Gabon, to visit the hospital of Dr. Albert Schweitzer. George's mother came back with him, and she spent our last month in Africa with the family.

It was with mixed emotions that we left old friends in the jungle, as well as new friends in Kinshasa, when we left Africa. As far as I was concerned, that was the end of an interesting period in our lives. However, for some reason, the hospital in the middle of the jungle was not to be forgotten, for the best was yet to come. My last letter from Africa to my mother expressed my excitement about coming home after two years:

June 6th

Dearest Mother & Bob,

Perhaps this will be my last letter home since we are planning to leave Kinshasa June 16th. As of now out plans are to arrive in Nashville on June 30th. I think our flight from New York arrives around 2:00 a.m. in the morning!!

Our tentative plans are to first fly to Nairobi, Kenya for a few days. This is in East Africa (not Congo) and George & Mama B. and the big ones will spend a night at "Treetops" watching the animals. From Kenya we will fly to Egypt to view the pyramids and Sphinx. Then on to my part of the trip—Switzerland! I wanted one last look at the Alps (you have to see them to believe them!) We plan to arrive in Zurich, rent a Volks bus and drive to Lucerne for a few days. We want to drive over one or two routes we did summer before last one more time!

We are busy packing those trunks again! I'm bringing a few treasures in my hand so if the trunks make it, O.K., if not O.K.!! Better close and get to work. School is out this week so I'll not have as much time then. Several doctors are giving us a formal affair Sat. night so I plan to use my white formal!

Love to you both and see you soon.

Barbara

We packed up in June of 1971 and headed for home. We planned a few weeks of travel before landing in Nashville, and as we left the Kinshasa airport, I counted six children, mother, father, grandmother, and twenty-two pieces of luggage. Our journey home took us to our first stop, Nairobi, Kenya. Nairobi is a cosmopolitan city, and the population speaks English, which makes it hard to believe one is still in Africa.

We stayed at a Mennonite guest house for several days while we toured the area. George, Mrs. Burrus, Lisa, Laura, and Roger took a side trip to "Treetops," a game reserve near Nairobi. The hotel was built on stilts and the rooms were high up in the trees. It was built around a watering hole, and you could observe the animals coming for water in their natural habitat. Small children were not allowed, so the three younger girls and I stayed at the guest house in Nairobi. "Treetops" was the place where Princess Elizabeth was informed of her father's death and prepared to return to England as the queen.

From Nairobi, we flew to Cairo, Egypt. A Mennonite travel agency in Kinshasa booked our journey home, and since they were also friends, we trusted their plans. We landed in Cairo at two in the morning and boarded a bus for our hotel, the Lotus Hotel. The first stop was an old boarded-up hotel, which looked deserted. Imagine my surprise when the driver said, "First stop—Lotus Hotel!" We all piled out about the time that George realized he had no Egyptian money. Out of the shadows stepped a man who paid the driver and introduced himself as Solomon.

Our family on camels with a view of the Sphinx.

He went into the hotel with us and helped us wake up the manager, who in turn woke up the crew, who in turn dressed in their long robes and fez caps to put sheets on the beds! How we were ever booked into the Lotus Hotel is still a mystery! To call it a hotel is exaggerating, since it was unkempt, no screens on the windows, and very strange.

Mrs. Burrus and I had already decided we could not spend a week in such surroundings, so we sent George out very early the next morning to find a suitable place. As he walked through the lobby, there sat Solomon offering his assistance again. We went from the ridiculous to the sublime, and George got us a suite at the Nile Hilton, a beautiful hotel overlooking the Nile River. I was not sure how we could afford it, but enjoy it we did. When we moved into the suite, there was a large bouquet of fresh flowers awaiting us, and the card simply said, "Solomon."

As the week progressed, Solomon proved to be a friend indeed. He had a large old four-door Cadillac, with driver, waiting for us each morning for a day of sightseeing and unbelievable adventure.

We traveled to Alexandria, a port on the beautiful Mediterranean Sea, and visited the palace of King Farouk. Another day, we drove to Memphis, said to be the oldest city in civilization, and the site of very old statues. The children enjoyed our day in an area outside of Cairo called Giza. Here one finds the Pyramids of Giza and the Sphinx. The entire family rode camels from the Pyramids down to the Sphinx and beheld one of the Seven Wonders of the World. Personally, I was somewhat disappointed in the Sphinx, since the nose was damaged from the days of Napoleon's battles.

After that, we rode back to a tent in the desert behind the Pyramids and had afternoon tea. While George, Mrs. Burrus, Solomon, and I enjoyed tea, the children galloped around the tent on camels. That night, we attended the "Sound and Lights" show featuring the Sphinx and Pyramids.

Solomon worked for a travel agency in Cairo, and maybe he was looking for us the night we arrived. Who knows? He cautioned me about buying souvenirs in the hotel and, instead, took us to his cousin's shop! We purchased a brass and wood coffee table to be shipped home. One day he took us down into the teeming city for a visit to a perfume shop and its small factory behind the showroom. We also visited the Cairo museum and viewed King Tut's exhibition. Years later, Kate wanted to go to Chicago to see the exhibition like her friend when we reminded her about seeing it in Cairo, Egypt.

I remarked in a casual way to Solomon about the lovely blue crystal ashtrays in the Nile Hilton rooms. As we boarded the plane for Switzerland, Solomon handed me two packages. In one were some Egyptian sweets, and in another, six beautiful ashtrays from the Nile Hilton. I accepted them in good faith. The week was so delightful that we felt like there must be a hitch in Solomon's plans, and we were sure when our table did not arrive until the following February. This was due to a dock strike in New York, so Solomon proved to be a good friend who made our time in Egypt such a fascinating week.

From Egypt, we flew to Zurich, and we spent a few days in one of my favorite haunts, Lucerne. Mrs. Burrus and I took advantage of going to a beauty salon, and she begged me to have a touch-up. In the two years away from Nashville, some gray hairs were appearing. However, I had earned these and wanted them left intact.

From Switzerland, we headed home and arrived in Nashville the first of July 1971. We were met by members of both families, and it was a grand homecoming after two years. As we left the Nashville airport, I counted three adults, six children, and twenty-two pieces of luggage!

Chapter 4

Travels with the Burruses

After our return from Africa in 1971, I felt as if I wanted to stay in Nashville for the rest of my life. Nevertheless, many trips to interesting places lay ahead for George and me. The following are some descriptions and details of such journeys.

In 1972, George and I went to the islands of Trinidad and Barbados. What a contrast these two places represent! Trinidad was somewhat more tropical and reminded me of Africa on a small scale, while Barbados was a small paradise of white sand and blue water. We had gone to a medical meeting in Trinidad and only stopped at Barbados for three days. We enjoyed some snorkeling, and George tried the scuba diving course.

The year 1975 was one of a great camping adventure in Europe. Our group of twenty-four included our family of eight, my sister Gayle and her daughter, Kim, my nieces, Jennye Dale Burrus and Lynn Castleman, my mother, George's mother, and two other families. Dr. and Mrs. Arnold Killen took their three daughters and Lucy's mother, and Dr. and Mrs. Robert Youngblood took their two children. As I think back on the trip, there were too many people and more responsibility than anyone needed!

We flew to Frankfurt, Germany, from New York and picked up four Volkswagen campers for our two-week trip. Each camper had some beds, a table, and a stove for cooking. We carried extra tents for some of the older children. George planned to drive one camper, Dr. Killen would drive one, Dr. Youngblood would drive his family, and we hoped that Lisa, Laura, and Jennye Dale could drive the fourth camper. However, we found that they needed to be twenty-one in order to be covered by insurance. So that left only Mama Barbara to drive the stick shift Volkswagen camper for two weeks in Europe! Sometimes the memory of that trip seems like a big black cloud over me, but I tried to adjust and be a sport.

We left Frankfurt in a caravan of four large campers, two red and two orange in color. We stayed in official campgrounds, and our first night was spent in Heidelberg, Germany, by the Rhine River. The next morning we toured the University of Heidelberg and headed for the border of Czechoslovakia. At that time, Czechoslovakia was behind the Iron Curtain, and we were very careful about cameras and too much talk. Someday, I would like to return to the city of Prague and focus on the beautiful old buildings and other attributes of this marvelous old city.

I was barely keeping my head above water by driving and paying attention to George's red camper in front of me. However, a red light caught my vehicle, and I looked off instead of looking ahead to George's car as he passed on after a green light. Arnold Killen and Bob Youngblood were following me, so the three campers were separated from the lead one driven by George. Seven or eight children were riding in George's camper since he carried a large bag of candy with him.

The three remaining campers parked in a large square surrounding a beautiful cathedral and shops. As we browsed the shops, I was beginning to be concerned since I had all the passports in my possession. We had planned to leave Czechoslovakia through the border at Bratislava, and no passports would present a problem. We decided to go to the American Embassy to report a missing American, no passports, and a car full of children. I will always remember the words of an aide in the ambassador's office. He said, "Lady, you have a problem." After a few hours, we decided to move on and return to our campers in the square.

To our extreme delight and surprise, we counted four campers parked and knew that George and the children were close by somewhere. We found them in an ice cream parlor, and they said that we were the ones lost most of the day!

We left Prague and drove into the countryside to camp and meet some of the people. One evening, we shared a campfire with some young people. We felt that their speech was guarded, and they seemed somewhat tense. They asked many questions about the United States.

Our group left the border between Czechoslovakia and Austria at Bratislava as planned. We looked forward to Austria and all of the beauty in this country's mountains and meadows. Our first night's camping was in the historical city of Vienna. The men agreed to babysit with the children under twelve while the ladies and young folks took a night tour of Vienna. The highlight of that tour was a presentation of Vienna's lovely costumed dancers waltzing to the "Blue Danube Waltz."

We journeyed on to Salzburg, and here the children took a "Sound of Music" tour. This great movie was filmed in and around Salzburg, and they visited sights like the home of the Von Trapps and the gazebo used in the film.

Our next stop was in Munich, Germany, and the big thrill there was a McDonald's restaurant. The children could hardly contain themselves until we agreed to stop for lunch. Remember now, we were four Volkswagen campers traveling in some sort of order. Every night we stopped to cook our meal and sleep in one of the many campgrounds in Europe.

Before leaving Germany, I once again missed a turnoff that George made, so Arnold Killen's camper and my camper were alone on the German autobahn. I needed to stop and talk with Arnold, so I pulled off the autobahn and parked in the grass. Soon two German policemen appeared and fined us forty dollars, or eighty marks, for being on the grass. It made better sense to get off the busy highway, but what could we do?

From Germany, we passed into the beautiful and pristine country of Switzerland. Next to England, I prefer the Swiss mountains, meadowlands, and lakes of this very small country. Zurich and Lucerne were lovely cities, and we camped outside Lucerne. That evening, we treated the group to a real Swiss meal complete with entertainment by a live

Swiss band and the famous horn blowers. I made the acquaintance of a shopkeeper in Lucerne, and over the years have bought cuckoo clocks and Hummel figures from Portia's shop.

Back in 1969, we had discovered a very small campground in Innertkirchen, Switzerland, and we wanted our family and friends to see it. It was in the backyard of a chalet close by a stream and small railway. The railway had one small car that ran between Innertkirchen and Meiringen, a small village of wood carvers. The children enjoyed playing in the stream and taking a short train ride to Meiringen for a treat.

Another treat in Switzerland was going to Zermatt, a skiing village high in the mountains. We boarded a train for the trip since no cars are allowed in the village, and the train was met by horse-drawn sleighs. We boarded gondolas that took us up to a higher altitude and we viewed the famous mountain, Matterhorn.

Reluctantly, we left Switzerland and drove toward Paris. We camped outside Paris at the Versailles campgrounds. Before going into Paris, we toured the Versailles Palace, home of King Louis XIV. It was here that the peace treaty of World War I was signed in the "Hall of Mirrors." We decided to use only two campers for our drive into Paris. That proved to be an excellent idea, because I do not think I would have made it driving in the city of many cars with everyone in a hurry. We toured Notre Dame, the Eiffel Tower, the Arc de Triomphe, and the Louvre Museum. Years later, I would return to those places many times, but for now I was giving our group a tourist's tour.

From Paris we headed toward Belgium and the city of Brussels. We took the group to 66 Avenue Colonial and a view of the row house where we lived in 1969 before going to Africa. The children enjoyed showing their cousins, grandmothers, aunt, and friends the neighborhood near our house. We took a side trip to Brugge, a medieval city of lace makers. Canals wind throughout the city, and we took a boat tour in the canals.

From Brussels, we drove on to Frankfurt, Germany, to board our plane for home. I was so relieved to turn in my camper and give up the job of chauffeur. There is one thing to say of this trip; I will never forget it!

The following pages reflect some detailed views of the trip prepared by our great friend, Arnold Killen:

Our good traveling friends, Lucy and Arnold Killen, with Barbara.

Tuesday, June 10, 1975

Started early this a.m. and had a beautiful drive along the Neckar River to Stuttgart, a great industrial city and also a leading cultural center. We went through the Mercedes Benz factory—an immense place and very interesting.

In the afternoon we found a campground which was run by a typical German family, then went to the grocery and had lunch.

It is now raining but we hope it will be only a shower—have had good weather until this rain.

Wednesday, June 11th

We are getting an early start today, headed for Rothenberg, stopped to shop for our groceries. It is interesting to hear the Germans speak, and our men can communicate enough to get by. Susan Killen is putting her German into practice.

The sun is out, a good day and the scenery beautiful. We have gotten on the Romantic Road at the City of Nordlingen, and our destination for today will be Rothenberg on the Tauber.

This old, old city is like a story-book-land place, narrow cobblestone streets with tall-gabled houses and colorful flower boxes at all of the windows. The homes were neat and clean and the countryside well kept. The architecture has kept its 16th century appearance.

A group of us climbed to the top of the great stone wall around the city, used for protection at one time. An old church built in the 15th century was also a point of interest.

Our campground was very good and all of the scenery in Germany was most beautiful. We will be getting back into Germany later.

Thursday, June 12th

We crossed the border into Czechoslovakia this afternoon and it took about an hour to get through with our visas, passports, etc. Quite a contrast to Germany!

Our campground was at Pilsen where a group of young people were camping. One of the girls who could speak a little English played her guitar and we all sang—Arnold Killen and Lisa Burrus also played us a tune. All of our young people commented on how much they enjoyed this experience with the Czech young folks. (I hear Arnold Killen has been receiving cards from his "pen-pal.")

Friday, June 13th

What a day! We drove on to Prague, the capital. George Burrus and his campers got separated from us, but we found them later in the day at one of the sidewalk cafes. Our visit to the American Embassy was interesting and also to a beautiful Cathedral at which a wedding had just taken place. The bride and groom and family were on the outside being photographed, and cars decorated in a festive manner were waiting.

Later—We are now walking over the oldest bridge in Europe still in use (for walking only), very wide with cobblestones, many statues all along the way and the Vltava River below. Prague is a very large city—many people walking, some adults riding bicycles, babies being pushed in buggies, and cars driving very fast. (Gas $2.50 a gallon.)

We are camping in a small place tonight and have had dinner at a restaurant where they led us to the second floor—the first floor was a little too noisy for us! A very simple meal cooked on a coal stove.

Saturday, June 14th

We left our campground this a.m., but stopped to wait for one of our campers who had gone back to get an article left behind.

A young, attractive girl who spoke German wanted a ride to a small town we would be passing. (She lives in "Czech" but was born in Frankfurt, Germany.) Arnold communicated with her and seemed to enjoy their conversation. When we reached her destination, she waved and said "auf Wiedersehen."

Tonight we will be camping at Bratislava, a very large city on the Danube River. The Czech people are celebrating their 30th year under the Socialistic regime.

Sunday, June 15th

We are now on our way to Vienna, Austria, just drove over the beautiful Blue Danube. Suddenly we come upon the mountains and are passing many hills of wild red poppies—beautiful. Stopped to help a car which was stuck in the mud.

After a very good lunch in an attractive restaurant, we saw some of the sights in Vienna and then drove to our campsite.

All of the ladies and three of the older girls went on an evening sightseeing tour which was beautiful.

We made our first stop at a restaurant for chicken soup and wine; then drove to the outdoor concert hall where we heard beautiful Viennese music played in a lovely setting—waltzes by three young couples were enjoyable.

After the concert, we made our next stop at an outdoor restaurant where we were served a plate of cold cuts, cheese, and rye bread with wine. (Ask Gayle if she remembers the Canadian gentleman who was very attentive.)

Vienna with all the gardens, parkways, and lights was a beautiful sight in the evening. The Voltz Church with its twin steeples all lighted was lovely.

Monday, June 16th

Leaving for Salzburg, Austria, stopped at Melk, a small picturesque town in Austria, narrow winding streets, an old monastery which is now a school—also an old church with a cemetery adjoining it, graves dating from the 11th Century.

We had a good campground for the night, but "too bad," we had rain at dinner time and all night.

Tuesday, June 17th

(Approaching Salzburg, Beth Killen got a lovely picture of white sailboats on the blue, blue water.) Drove into Salzburg this morning, went sightseeing and enjoyed this old, old city with beautiful old buildings and lots of sidewalk cafes.

We visited Mozart's birthplace, and his statue was very imposing in the center of a large square of old buildings. Some of the group enjoyed visiting the setting where the "Sound of Music" was filmed.

While sightseeing we met a couple from Kansas City (strangers to us), who had been visiting his father in a town south of Vienna—we chatted with them and got their address.

Now leaving Salzburg on our way to Munich, scenery beautiful with some snow-covered mountains. (Beth Killen trying to get some good shots from time to time.)

We just crossed the border and are again viewing the most beautiful scenery, mountains, and valleys. Munich, the capital of Bavaria, is the gateway to the Bavarian Alps, a glorious land of ice blue lakes, picturesque mountain villages and snow-clad peaks.

It is raining again, but enjoying the drive, had supper at McDonald's (seemed like home) and then went to the campground for the night.

Wednesday, June 18th

After a good warm shower, cooking our breakfast, and doing some washing, we left Munich and are now on our way to Fussen. Our group visited the Concentration Camp in Dachau, Germany, in which at least 30,000 prisoners died during the Nazi regime. Very depressing. We later stopped at Augsburg for lunch at a German restaurant.

Thursday, June 19th

Last night we spent a cold, rainy night in a most beautiful spot, and today went through an old castle, "Neuschwanstein," drove through gorgeous mountains, valleys, and small villages—wonderful scenery!

The castle was begun in 1869 by Ludwig II who lived in it only 102 days. In 1886 he was deposed by the Governmental Commission sent from Munich, and he died three days later. There are views of the mountains and waterfalls from the castle windows.

One unusual aspect of the interior is an artificial stalactite grotto with a small adjoining winter garden, which recalls the Tannhauser legend, and the great chamber whose decor has for its theme the legend of Lohengrin. Ludwig II had been a patron of Richard Wagner.

Spent the night at Lindenberg, a lovely place. Still in Germany, but on our way to Switzerland. Stopped in the little country of Liechtenstein and had tea and coffee—could see many old castles on this mountainous drive.

Friday, June 20th

Arrived at Lucerne, Switzerland (on a beautiful lake), a lovely city with the "old look" and flowers everywhere. We enjoyed all the shops and had dinner at a Swiss restaurant, delicious food and very lively Swiss music—yodeling and playing the long Swiss horn. Our campground was a most beautiful setting.

Saturday, June 21st

After breakfast this morning, we did a little washing and then got started on another shopping spree—the linen shops were especially attractive. Spent our first night at Innertkirchen—a lovely spot in the valley with the Swiss Alp Mountains on all sides, some snow-covered peaks. In the setting of one little chalet, you could just see the story of "Heidi" taking place.

Sunday and Monday, June 22nd & 23rd

Spent our second and third nights in this glorious spot—Innertkirchen. We drove to a higher altitude and had lunch at a nice restaurant while some of our group hiked up still higher. It began to rain and they came in soaking wet—but enjoyed it.

Tuesday, June 24th

Left early today and caught the train (Europe's highest mountain railway, 10,132 ft.) to Zermatt, an outstanding winter sports resort which offers the skier an unprecedented variety of glorious tours and runs until late in springtime. In the splendour of this proudest 13,000 ft. peak, the Matterhorn, which has been named "The King of the Mountains," Zermatt is located at an altitude of 5,265 ft. A chairlift takes one up to 7,478 ft., and a steep ropeway rises to 9,820 ft.

The trip took most of the day and the panoramic view of the mountains, valleys, and gorges from the train was breathtaking.

After our return trip, we drove on some distance and had good camping facilities at Aarburg.

Switzerland, with the beauty and grandeur of the Swiss Alps, and all the charm of the countryside, little villages, and chalets, was a high point of our trip.

Wednesday, June 25th

Had breakfast, got packed up and left very early on our way to Paris, France. We are now going through Germany again, beautiful scenery, crossed the border at noon over the Rhine River—came directly into Strasbourg. Stopped for lunch and passed an old, old cemetery. Camped at Versailles out of Paris in a wooded area. Very primitive plumbing!

Thursday, June 26th

We spent the day seeing some of the interesting sights in Paris; Arc de Triomphe, Eiffel Tower, the Louvre, University of Paris, and the Seine River. The night view of the Eiffel Tower, with fountains all lighted in the background, was a lovely sight. We enjoyed very much having dinner at a Chinese restaurant, "The Pearl of China." (We could not do justice to Paris in one day, but this part of our trip was an after-thought.)

Friday, June 27th

Left this a.m., our destination Frankfurt, Germany. Before leaving Versailles, we visited the summer palace of King Louis XIV with its formal gardens. There was much grandeur found here—beautiful old marble, gold leaf, oil murals on the walls and ceiling, tapestries covering some of the walls, and busts of all the important leaders of the French Army over a period of many centuries.

Late in the afternoon went across the border into Belgium, found a camping area near Brussels, and the children and older girls stopped for hamburgers which they had been so anxious to find.

The older girls stayed with the younger ones while we went out for a delicious dinner at an attractive French restaurant—beautiful flowers and the dinner served formally. We chatted with the manager, who was a very polished and hospitable gentleman. He offered to show us around the next morning, but we had to get an early start for Frankfurt.

Saturday, June 28th

Left this morning at 7:00, hoping to reach Frankfurt shortly after noon. Stopped at the former home of the Burrus family (while they were in Brussels for four months before going to Africa) and visited with their friends.

We stopped at Waterloo, near Brussels, where the Battle of Waterloo was fought in 1815 which ended Napoleon's power forever.

When we reached Frankfurt, we turned in our campers at the rental place which took a while. We then had dinner and spent the night at a German "Gasthaus" (Guest House)—a delightful place with rooms, baths, showers, etc., clean and convenient.

Sunday, June 29th

How great it was to have a bathtub and a good night's sleep and start out this morning refreshed after a good breakfast! The German family who ran the Guest House was so very hospitable and accommodating.

We are now on the Lufthanse, having a good flight and will arrive in New York about 5:00 p.m. Then after a layover in New York, the Killens and Frances Bennett on to Kansas City; the Burrus party on to Nashville; and the Youngbloods to their home in Wilson, N.C.

All in all, our European trip was most interesting and delightful, and was an experience which we shall always remember as "something special."

(Thanks to the Youngbloods and the Burrus family for preparing such good breakfasts and other meals!)

The meals we had in restaurants were also very good and Pomme Frites (French Fries) and Cokes, generally without ice, were available at most restaurants on our trip.

(Thanks to the three men, George, Bob, and Arnold, and Barbara Burrus for doing such a good job of driving the campers, especially in Paris where the traffic and the pattern of driving was unbelievable.)

In 1977, we planned a camping trip to Canada and the New England coast. The Killen family accompanied us, and again, our three older children, Lisa, Laura, and Roger, had summer jobs. We flew to Toronto, rented two campers, and set out to Montreal and Quebec City. The Old Fort and quaint horse-drawn carriages added a flare to this French city. We traveled on to Maine and enjoyed a sailboat ride in beautiful Bar Harbor. We visited Cape Cod and Martha's Vineyard outside Boston Harbor. We rented mopeds and covered the interesting spots for tourists. The children enjoyed Plymouth and a tour of the *Mayflower*. Wax statues on the *Mayflower* helped to bring alive the journey of our first Pilgrims. We pressed on to Buffalo, New York, to view Niagara Falls. Reading about Niagara Falls is not the same as standing at the site of this magnificent wonder. We were reluctant to leave the beautiful site, but returned to Toronto to return our campers and fly back to Nashville.

My fascination with the British Isles began back in 1969 as we made our way to India. Since that date, we have returned many times to different sections of Great Britain. On our way to India, we took the route from London northwest to the Cotswolds, Stratford-upon-Avon, Wales, Blackpool, and on to Liverpool, a port on the west coast.

In 1978, we planned a trip to Great Britain with our close friends, Lucy and Arnold Killen, their three girls, Beth, Susan, and Laura, and

Lucy's mother, "Memaw." We took our three daughters, Kate, Nan, and Barbara, and George's mother, Mrs. Burrus. Our three other children, Lisa, Laura, and Roger, had summer jobs at home.

We flew to Scotland, picked up a van for twelve persons, and headed on our way. Instead of camping, we tried bed-and-breakfast. We found this to be our favorite mode of travel. However, finding rooms for twelve persons took a long time each afternoon, and we spent more time in the morning picking up all the passengers.

Our trip took us north to a small island off the coast of Scotland called the Isle of Skye. We put our van on the ferry and rode across with it. Not many people inhabited the small island; however, we found a quaint guest house and spent the night. We were most impressed with the lush vegetable and flower gardens tended by the owners of the small hotel. We enjoyed teatime and visiting with other guests from around the world.

Our journey took us to Glasgow and Edinburgh for some limited sightseeing before going south into England. The Scottish countryside is picturesque with very narrow roads and lay-bys. A lay-by is an area by the side of the road where a car stops for another car coming from the opposite direction to pass.

George and Arnold enjoyed a bit of history, viewing Hadrian's Wall. This wall was built by the Romans to protect them from the Scots who were fierce warriors. Within the English borders, we traveled to York to view the York Minster, a cathedral built from 1250 to 1330 and a magnificent structure. Our route was central England, and we passed through Nottingham, Coventry, Oxford, and into the Cotswolds. Someday, I would like to spend a month or so in the Cotswolds, which means rolling hills. The story of the Cotswolds is really the story of wool. For much of the Middle Ages, Cotswold wool was exported throughout Europe, bringing wealth to the region. Some favorite towns in this area are Chipping Campden, Stow-on-the-Wold, Burton-on-the-Water, Upper and Lower Slaughter, Woodstock, and Broadway.

We again toured the grounds of Blenheim Palace, and I vowed to go inside someday. But that would have to wait.

The second week of our trip took us by ferry overnight to the Hock of Holland. We picked up two vehicles and set out to visit Amsterdam, the home of Anne Frank, Brussels, where we again visited 66 Avenue Colonial, our home in 1969 in Belgium, and Brugge, the lace-making center of the world. Before leaving Brussels, I slipped away one day from a hotel near the Grand-Place and purchased a wedding veil for my five daughters to wear one day in the future.

Our plane for the trip home would leave from Paris, so we made our way into the section of France called Normandy. We visited Omaha Beach, one of the D-day beaches in World War II, and the American Cemetery. One of my favorite places to visit on this trip was Mont-Saint-Michel, an island rising out of the water looking much like Cinderella's castle. Winding streets full of shops, people, and wares encircled the island until you reached the top of the mountain, site of the monastery and church. Before we left from Paris for our journey home, we ate at George's favorite Chinese restaurant, The Pearl of China, in Paris, France.

In 1980 and 1982, we had two trips with the Denton Cooley Society, a group of his residents through the years. The first trip in 1980 was to Rio de Janeiro, Brazil. Rio de Janeiro held such sights as Sugar Loaf Mountain, Ipanema Beach, and lush jungle waterfalls with rare orchids and other flowers. The side trip to view the "Christ of the Andes" was very meaningful after having seen the pictures. Some parts of Rio de Janeiro reminded me of Zaire, the conditions of some of its people plus the hot tropical climate.

The trip in 1982 was to Athens, Greece, and a three-day boat cruise of some of the islands. We visited the Acropolis, which in Greek means "city at the top of a hill." Upon this hill stands the ruins of the Parthenon, which represents the peak of the Greek Doric style of architecture.

One interesting activity of the meeting was a tennis tournament planned by Dr. Cooley. George made it to the finals, and he and his partner opposed Dr. Cooley and his partner. Either Dr. Cooley overestimated the skill of his partner, or George underestimated the skill of his. However, at the banquet, Dr. Cooley had the opportunity to award the trophy to George and his partner.

George and Dr. Denton A. Cooley at a banquet after a friendly tennis tournament. George won!

After our meeting in Athens was over, we boarded a cruise ship and sailed out into the beautiful Aegean Sea. Our first island was Mikonos, noted for good shopping and unusual wares. Between the islands, we enjoyed the relaxing atmosphere and spectacular buffets on the ship. The presentation of the food was a daily occupation of the camera buffs! George enjoyed the island of Kos where Hippocrates, the father of medicine, practiced under the plane tree four hundred years B.C. The tree is forty-feet in circumference. My favorite island was Santorini. The town was built on a hill high above the blue waters of the Aegean Sea. The dwellings were white stucco, and the combination of colors was more vivid than any painted picture. To reach the town or village, one had to ride a donkey up many steps or ride a cable car. George chose the donkey, and I willingly rode the cable car. Our last island was Rhodes. Standing near the harbor entrance is the famous Colossus, a statue of Helios (the sun). This cruise of the Greek Isles was a relaxing and refreshing trip in the calm Aegean Sea.

Each time that we camped, we seemed to have fewer persons, plus the fact that our children were older and too involved to leave home. In 1983, Lucy, Arnold, George, and I took some two-man pop-up tents and went to a medical meeting in Innsbruck, Austria. While in Innsbruck for the meeting, we stayed in an old hotel, and Lucy and I spent our days browsing the shops for Austrian treasures. We especially like the traditional Austrian Geiger jackets, which we purchased for our girls. Before the meeting, we had landed in Brussels and made our way south toward

Bastogne, Belgium, site of the Battle of Bastogne during World War II. We viewed the monument of Americans killed in that famous battle, and then on to Luxembourg, the largest and most southerly of the nine provinces of Belgium.

For old time's sake, we drove by the little campground in Innertkirchen, Switzerland, and as we turned toward Austria, we stopped at St. Moritz to view this skiing mecca.

After the meeting, we drove to Munich and left from Frankfurt to cross the ocean homeward bound. On that trip Lucy and I said, "No more camping." From now on, it is bed-and-breakfast!

In 1984, we returned to London, England, for a meeting with the Denton Cooley Society. George and I landed in London a week before the meeting began, and we rented a small car to tour. We drove west toward Cornwall and the rugged coast. We passed through Plymouth and Penzance and on to Land's End, the most southern point of English soil. On our way to Land's End, we passed rolling hills with sheep grazing and scenes of pastoral beauty. A small museum stands high above the rugged coastline, with memorabilia of days past, including U-boats from World War II.

We spent the night at a bed-and-breakfast dairy farm. George and the owner shared dairyman stories with the owner bemoaning the introduction of cheap dairy products from the continent. The house was very old with high ceilings, and that evening, we sat in the parlor visiting with the family. This is the way to know people in other cultures, not staying in a big hotel. However, I must admit I always enjoyed the service in a grand hotel such as the Ritz in Paris or the Nile Hilton in Cairo.

After leaving Cornwall, we drove once again to the Cotswolds. I purchased a biography of Princess Anne, since I would have the opportunity to meet her in London. The princess was coming to a reception as the guest of Dr. Cooley, and we met and talked briefly. She was charming, and a few years later, she came to Nashville for a benefit. I did not go because after all I had already made her acquaintance.

In 1989, we traveled to England and Ireland. By that time, all of our children were grown, and the same was true for the Killens and

Youngbloods. We planned an easy bed-and-breakfast trip for six, and we enjoyed our friends of internship days. We left London and traveled toward the south of England, stopping to view the white cliffs of Dover, made famous during World War II, as we sang about peace coming to England. We also viewed the construction of the famous Channel Tunnel linking England and France.

From there we traveled to Brighton, Portsmouth, Bristol, and around the port area of Pembroke. We boarded a ferry that also carries cars and rode across St. George's Channel on the rough Irish Sea. I had to think of other more pleasant visions than my Irish Sea trip in 1969 on the way to India. Many people on board were very sick. Our ferry docked at Wexford, and we were on Irish soil. The first town we visited was Waterford, famous for crystal. We watched with fascination as the glass-blowers formed beautiful bowls, goblets, and other treasures.

At the end of the tour, we were led into a room of Waterford. Chandeliers, tables, goblets, bowls, clocks, and many more treasures tempted the tourist. Lucy, Melba, and I were reluctant to leave, but we needed to continue our view of Ireland. We followed the Ring of Kerry, a southwest tour of the coastline. Rock fences were evident throughout the countryside, and small thatched-roof huts dotted the land. The best food was available in the Irish pub, which served as a social center for each town.

I was anxious to get back on English soil, and we completed our Irish tour and sailed back over the Irish Sea. Our trip back was somewhat calmer, much to our delight. Once again, I had to pass through the Cotswolds, especially Broadway and Upper Slaughter. In Upper Slaughter, there is a truly English inn called Lord of the Manor. We spent a lovely evening there, first with an appetizer in front of the fire in the drawing room and then a splendid English meal in the dining room. "I shall return," were my thoughts as we drove away that evening.

Lucy, Arnold, George, and I planned a trip to Israel in the spring of 1993, but changed our minds due to the country's instability. Instead, we chose to visit some new spots in France and some old favorites in

Switzerland. We flew to Zurich and introduced Lucy and Arnold to our special place, the Wolfsprung. Remon Beffa was as usual the genial host and excellent chef in the kitchen. We stayed two nights at the lovely chalet on Lake Lucerne. We drove into Lucerne and reminisced about our 1975 camping outside of Lucerne. Reluctantly, we left the Wolfsprung and drove south to Genoa, Italy. We then drove along the Cote d'Azur, viewing such new places as Monte Carlo in the tiny principality of Monaco, Nice, and Cannes. The favorable climate, the grandeur of the rugged costal scenery, and the blue Mediterranean Sea made this trip very pleasant indeed. We then headed north toward Grenoble, France, on to Zurich, and one last night at the Wolfsprung.

George's brother, Swan, a doctor in Tupelo, Mississippi, retired in April of 1995. We had discussed a trip upon his retirement with him and his wife, Marianne. We left Nashville the end of May in 1995 and flew to London. We rented a Honda station wagon and traveled toward Norfolk or East Anglia on the east coast. The area was new to George and me, and we were anxious to explore another area of England. I have always enjoyed reading English history and especially any material about the present queen, Elizabeth II. To my surprise, we passed a sign pointing to Sandringham, one of the royal residences. It was open to the public at that time of year, and my fellow passengers indulged my choice of visiting that day. As we entered the large ornate gate, we purchased a guide book published by the Estate Office, Sandringham, Norfolk. The introduction is as follows:

"Dear old Sandringham, the place I love better than anywhere else in the world." So wrote King George V, who had known it for as long as he could remember, and for whom it was, above all, home. King George VI's affection for it was no less keen. "I have always been so happy here," he wrote to Queen Mary, "and I love the place." King Edward VII, its first royal occupant, had made it a glittering centre of society during the forty-nine years that he owned it, and transformed the shooting into some of the finest in the country.

Christmas used to be the great occasion at Sandringham, and it was here that King George V made his first Christmas broadcast in 1932. It was also at Sandringham that twenty-five years later, Her Majesty the

Standing in front of Sandringham—Marianne, George, and Barbara.

Queen first made use of television for the same purpose. Nowadays, Her Majesty usually celebrates Christmas at Windsor Castle and moves to Sandringham for the New Year. We toured the family drawing rooms and dining room where I imagined the royal family gathering for their vacation. After our tour of the house, we walked over the grounds and viewed magnificent rhododendrons and azaleas. For me, it was already my favorite part of the trip.

Again, we entered Scotland and viewed miles of beautiful yellow fields of a product called rape seed. The land changed into rolling hills, which the Scots call moors. We spent our first night in Scotland in Dalhousie Castle. Our bed was draped in tartan material gathered into a crown at the top. Our meal that evening was by candlelight in a dungeon below the ground floor. So much for atmosphere.

Edinburgh was once more on our agenda, and thanks to Marianne and Swan, we took an extended tour of the Edinburgh Botanical Gardens and viewed yellow, red, white, purple, orange, and fuchsia rhododendrons.

Upon leaving Edinburgh, we traveled to St. Andrews, a famous golf course known to golfers around the world. We drove on north to

Aberdeen and then west to Inverness. Just short of Inverness, we stopped at the Culloden Battlefield. It was the site of the last battle on British soil. The conflict all started when Bonnie Prince Charles became of age, around twenty-five years, and came back to Scotland to reinstate himself on the British throne. The story was that the leaders of the Highland clans were not quite ready, but Prince Charles pushed them into going ahead and trying to overtake the English regulars. Gradually, the tide turned and the British regulars ran the Highlanders back into Scotland. At Culloden, they finished the Scottish army. Somehow, Prince Charles escaped back to Italy and Rome, never to return to Scotland.

The next day we took a bus and boat tour of Loch Ness. This is the largest freshwater lake in the British Isles, averaging some 750 feet deep. This is the lake with the history of people having sighted a dragon in the lake in the 1930s. On a hill beside the lake stands the ruins of Urquahart Castle. On an earlier visit when our children were smaller, they played within the ruins and claimed to have seen the monster of Loch Ness!

Once again back in England, we toured the Lake Country whose terrain is much more rolling and fairly fertile. We visited the homes of two famous people, William Wordsworth and Beatrix Potter. We went through the museum and cottage of William Wordsworth. He lived from 1770 to 1850 and was the Poet Laureate for the last seven years of his life.

We visited Hilltop, the home of Beatrix Potter, noted for her writing of children's stories, including ones about Peter Rabbit. She started at the age of thirty-three with illustrated letters to her former governess who at that time had six children. She was encouraged to get the illustrated letters published, and she personally had that done with 250 copies. The demand for copies was so great that the publisher published another 250 copies, and thereafter, the publishing snowballed. We saw the original sketches of her famous characters.

Our next visit was to the town of Stoke-on-Trent. We went to the Wedgewood factory and outlet store. It was fascinating to watch demonstrations of hand painting and decorating this beautiful china. This town is a center for the manufacture of fine English china.

We then drove on to Stratford-upon-Avon, home of William Shakespeare. We obtained tickets to the performance at the Royal

Shakespeare Theatre for *Taming of the Shrew*. It was a fantastic performance, and the fact that we were in Shakespeare's own territory made it all the more a real treat.

For the second time, we visited Warwick Castle. It was a fascinating place built in 1016. It has been recently privately owned by Madame Tussaud's corporation. She has a large waxworks in London and has put in lifelike statues in the castle depicting a royal hunting weekend. There is a statue of young Winston Churchill in one of the rooms, and the statues are clothed in beautiful costumes of the period.

George was attending a two-day meeting at the John Radcliff Hospital in Oxford, so Marianne, Swan, and I toured Oxford and the many colleges located there. We celebrated our forty-second anniversary with a special dinner at Lord of the Manor in Upper Slaughter on June 7, 1995, and on June 8, 1995 (our anniversary), we went to a gala reception inside Blenheim Palace. The palace was built by the Duke of Marlborough and was most famous in later years as the birthplace of Sir Winston Churchill. His mother, Jennie Jerome, from New York City married Lord Randolph Churchill and was visiting Blenheim Palace when the birth took place. "At Blenheim," Churchill once said, "I took two very important decisions: to be born and to marry. I am happily content with the decisions I took on both these occasions." A gentleman, playing the bagpipe, escorted us into the rooms of the palace, which were magnificent and filled with beautiful art and furnishings. The highlight of the reception was a performance by a military marching band in the quadrangle of the palace, complete with our National Anthem and fireworks. At last, I had experienced some of the magic of Blenheim Palace, which I first viewed in 1962 on our way to India.

I could not leave England without one or two more nights in my beloved Cotswolds. We browsed the antique shops, bookstores, and lovely tea rooms in Broadway (my favorite), and on our last evening, we dined at the Lygon Arms Hotel, a grand experience any time. I felt that Marianne and Swan enjoyed the trip as much as we did, and they were easy traveling companions.

CHAPTER 5

Bosobe, Zaire

Africa, 1985

As I sit here in the early morning, before the intense heat of an African day, it is a miracle that once again I find myself in this country of mystery and intrigue. During the summer of 1984, George began to talk about a return trip to Zaire. On our trip the previous summer to Sweden, Norway, Denmark, Finland, and Russia (Tallin), for a vacation, he had talked to Sven Ohm, the executive secretary of the Swedish Baptist Church, about going to Zaire in May of 1985. He had returned during June of 1980 with Lisa and Roger. His desire to be a doctor to those who "needed his talents" once again surfaced for him.

I was not really in favor of a return visit, if only for one month; however, any work so meaningful for George had to be a part of me. Kate wanted the chance to go with us in order to use her nursing skills, so with much hesitation in my heart, we departed Nashville on May 4, 1985.

We flew to Atlanta for one day with Laura and Charlie, our daughter and son-in-law, then overnight to Brussels, Belgium. Again, we visited the beautiful Grand-Place and reminisced at 66 Avenue Colonial. Kate wanted to take pictures of her early Belgian school. From there we flew on to Nigeria and landed in Kinshasa in the early morning of May 6, 1985.

We were met by a representative from the Swedish Baptists, and quickly passed through Customs and other business. At once, the sights, sounds, and smells of the country enveloped me! We were taken to the Methodist Presbyterian Hostel, where Laura had lived for about six months during 1969–1971. That afternoon, we went into the city of Kinshasa, a contrast of the new and old in Zaire, and visited the Ivory Market. George always enjoyed talking and trading with the men, but somehow my nature did not respond to this activity! We purchased malachite necklaces and bracelets as gifts, among which was a malachite elephant, a favorite treasure of mine.

The following morning a small plane took us up-country to the small village of Bosobe. We had lived and worked here in 1969, and it was with anticipation and curiosity that I returned. Shortly after arriving in Bosobe, I began to realize that God did not mean for me to carry the impressions of 1969–1971 always. My feelings and impressions were such a contrast, partly due perhaps to my being fifteen years older and, let's hope, somewhat wiser. In those early years, my main concerns had been my small children's health and education, whereas now I had the opportunity to observe and evaluate God's work and love being carried out by a small group of His children, Swedes, Zaireans, Indians, and Americans! I felt it was a gift for me to return.

For example, the visit was one of insight into some work being done by believers for the good of others needing help and healing. I saw first-hand how students in the nursing school were studying and trying to learn in order to assist their people. Through the Ellen Burrus Fund, we were to become a part of the construction for a new nursing building.

Another milestone since 1969 was the school for young girls who were learning to cut, sew, and sell clothes within the village. I marveled at how quickly they comprehended. I mentioned earlier about the airstrip and the events surrounding its construction. However, I realized now more than ever its importance for the work of Bosobe and its continuance into the future. How farsighted George was in this concept and reality of an airstrip for the people!

We arrive again in Bosobe in a small plane. We have known some of these friends since 1969.

Several incidents stand out during the three weeks of our visit to Bosobe. One was my hesitant introduction to the taste of crocodile. It was a cross between chicken and fish, and after a few bites, I needed no more! One delightful afternoon comes to mind. Missionaries in such isolated conditions tend to plan some outings to be an outlet for more communication. Such was the trip planned one Saturday afternoon, May 18. We all piled into a Land Rover and started off toward the Lukenie River, some ten miles away. After passing some African villages even more isolated than Bosobe, we arrived at the river. Such a beautiful sight! We rented an African pirogue that would accommodate all fifteen persons plus the African man to stand up and row the boat. But soon I noticed that two men were standing and rowing. One man's name was George Burrus. Who else?

We were heading for a sandbar up the river where we would swim and picnic. The pirogue ride gave me time to contemplate the scenery of river and jungle, as beautiful as Switzerland's meadow and mountain

River scene near Bosobe.

or Norway's fiord and mountain. The ride over and back was cool, refreshing, and gave me pause to remember . . . "Be still and know that I am God." On the way back, I observed that six languages were used or represented in the pirogue: Swedish, Hindi, French, English, and Lingala.

I had forgotten how many friends I had made in this small village in Zaire, only one country on the vast continent of Africa. They welcomed me back with sincere greetings and gifts. Moise (my trusted cook and friend of 1969) brought us papaya, grapefruit, and a live chicken. My former gardener's wife brought three eggs, and the Isai family brought peanuts and eggs. Fifteen years ago, a young girl named Esther had helped me take care of Barbara as a small baby and had lived with us in Kinshasa. Now at the age of thirty-one, she came to visit us with her small daughter of four years and to tell us she worked in the hospital pharmacy. You remember the stories about the chief of the tribe, his sons, the cookies, and the goat? This morning one of his sons came to visit and reminisce about his father's part in the airstrip.

Our days in Bosobe are fast drawing to a close, and I would like to describe one other scene for you. George, Kate, and I were invited for tea with the elders of the church one warm afternoon. After tea was served, we were welcomed and then asked for more help and assistance with the work here. Daddy answered, saying, "I don't really know why I'm here in Bosobe. Many curves in the path of life have brought me here. Here I am, and I hope to continue my affiliation with Bosobe and its work in the future." Maybe another part of God's plan will be to return to Bosobe for yet more work and support to these people, so far from my place of abode upon this earth!

George and I have enjoyed walking the airstrip in the late afternoon, and we always are greeted by the people . . . women with baskets full of wood or water balanced on their heads, and babies or wood on their backs. Yesterday, I witnessed a birth at the hospital attended by an African midwife. It was a real experience for me and one I will never forget.

I cannot complete my narrative about Bosobe without telling about some new friends from Sweden and India. We enjoyed our three weeks with the families Raju, Auxilles, Hellstein, and Pettersens. They opened their homes to us for fellowship, food, and help when needed.

After one month in Bosobe, I was ready to go home. The small airplane came for us, and even in my great anticipation to see everyone, plus Jessica, my only grandchild at the time, I felt that I was leaving a small part of my heart here. Maybe I felt that way because George loved it so much. As the plane climbed up over the African terrain, I wrote these few thoughts: "I feel a part of God's world community here at this time. The plan continues!"

We flew back to Geneva, Switzerland, and picked up a car for three days of sightseeing. After a month in the jungle, Kate, George, and I were ready for comfortable room and board. The first night we stayed near Geneva, at Hotel Du Loc, which means "by the lake." We ordered room service, and I remember well, we each had a chocolate sundae! The second night was in the town of William Tell's birthplace, and our accommodations were less pleasing. We stayed over a small local restaurant and bar, and the noise lasted most of the night.

Our favorite guest house—the Wolfsprung in Brunnen, Switzerland.

Kate and I decided to choose the place to stay our last night near Zurich. We were driving along when Kate asked her daddy to turn around and go back to a small hotel that we had passed. We will always give credit to Kate for finding the Wolfsprung for us. The Wolfsprung was a small guest house of eight or ten rooms for bed-and-breakfast. It was a Swiss Chalet on Lake Lucerne with the mountains of Switzerland on the other side of the lake. The owner, Remon Beffa, was a gourmet chef, and his gardens were perfection. Since that initial visit, we have returned some ten or twelve times and made a Swiss friend forever.

After our month in Bosobe in 1985, we returned to Zaire once or twice a year to carry supplies and help the people. Before 1990, we kept discarded hospital supplies in our upstairs, but after 1990, we had room at the farm for the large operation of packing boxes to carry to Zaire. The year 1991 stands out in my mind for two reasons, one interesting and the other reason unnerving!

I found this note in my journal:

The Chief Was My Guest
or
The Man Who Came to Dinner!

It was a cool rainy day in Sept. 1991. The place was Bosobe, Zaire. George and I had come back to the African hospital to bring medicine. The people were glad to see us because supplies and medicine were low! The chief of the region appeared at our door with a small goat for our meal. He was dressed in full tribal dress, complete with a large necklace of leopard's teeth, and carrying a dried elephant's tail.

Later, I heard the wailing of the goat and was told by our cook, Jacob, that he was told by the chief to cook it, and the chief, George, and I would enjoy it together! Of the three present, only one abstained.

We were certainly being cared for on this trip as I believe on all the other ones also, because we left on a Sunday night for home and in the early hours of Monday morning, the airport was seized and a coup took place. There were shooting, looting, and extreme unrest in the country. We heard about our close call when we reached Europe.

CHAPTER 6

Friends and Family

After we returned from Africa in 1971, the children fit right back into friendships and activities as if they had never been away. Lisa enrolled in Hillsboro High School as a sophomore and rode to school each day with Edie Graham. We had moved to 2103 Golf Club Lane in 1963 and were very fortunate in our next-door neighbors, the Ed Grahams. Betty B. and Ed Graham had five children, and their three youngest, John, Bebe, and Edie, spent many hours in our backyard playing with Lisa, Laura, Roger, and Kate.

In 1973, our friends, Harry and Shelley Page, invited us to go to Aspen, Colorado, for a ski trip. Little did we know what an impact the trip would have on our family. George took to skiing like a duck to water, but my efforts were more painful and sporadic. We would have breakfast and dinner with the Pages, but went about our own ways during the day since they were excellent skiers. After two days, Harry asked George where he had skied that day, and George replied, "Ruthie's Run." Harry said, "No way, George. It is one of the hardest runs on Aspen Mountain. I am going with you tomorrow!" He went with George the next morning and witnessed George skiing down Ruthie's Run.

Roger, Heidi Knaus, and Nan.

The next year we took the children and enjoyed staying at the Mountain Chalet in Snowmass. Our ski instructor for the family was Heidi Knaus from Switzerland, and the first time that I made it to the top was with Heidi and my good friend, Helen Alford.

In 1977, we purchased a condo on the slopes with three other families, Shelley and Dr. Harry Page, Helen and Dr. Bill Alford, and Doris and Dr. Harvey Bender. This move has proved to be a plus for family vacations, and four generations have enjoyed being together in Colorado. We usually go to a meeting in January and again in March with our family. I have skied all over Snowmass Mountain, but I finally admitted that it was not my cup of tea, and in the early 1990s, I retired. My children, George, and our grandchildren have continued to carry the ski banner.

From time to time, we saw famous stars in Snowmass and Aspen, and one day in particular stands out in my memory. We had invited Marian and Dr. Bill Stoney and Ellen and Dr. Bob Sadler to be our guests for the week.

Condo owners—Harry and Shelley Page, Helen and Bill Alford, Barbara and George Burrus, and Doris and Harvey Bender.

Since only the men skied down Aspen Mountain, we all were going to ride up in the gondola and have lunch, and the men would ski down while we women rode down. As we got into our gondola for the ride up, we saw Robert Wagner and Jill St. John getting into the gondola next to us.

We decided to try and get a picture with R. J. as we left the gondola at the top. Bill Stoney had his camera ready, and Ellen, Marian, and I were lined up on either side of R. J. Of course, his back was to the camera. About that time, Jill St. John said, "Turn around, R. J.," and when he did, we were smiling and ready for a picture. Later, Bill Stoney had the print blown up, and it stands framed on the wall of our condo.

Two favorite family vacation spots in addition to Snowmass, Colorado, have been Kiawah Island in South Carolina and the Grand Cayman Islands in the Caribbean Sea. In both spots, we rent condos on

Barbara, Robert Wagner, Ellen Sadler, and Marian Stoney.

the beach and enjoy fun, family, and fellowship.

Kiawah Island is near Charleston, South Carolina, and we enjoy this beautiful old southern historic town.

My favorite part of the Grand Cayman Islands is snorkeling and seeing all the beautiful fish below the water in every color. Some of the family enjoyed diving, but not me! George, Rufus Smith, and Charlie Smith dove one hundred feet down and made a tape of their dive. We enjoyed the tape—to each his own.

We had a fisherman friend in the Caymans named Vernal Ebanks, and we spent many fun days on his boat. His son would dive down, spear some fish and lobster, and Vernal would cook it all for our lunch. Talk about a fresh catch of the day!

Everyone should go to Hawaii at least once, if possible. We had good friends in Honolulu dating back to our Houston days, Lorraine and Dr. Richard Pang.

My farm workers in my favorite pose.

We attended the Western Thoracic Surgical Association meeting in Maui and stayed at the Grand Wailea Hotel right on the Pacific Ocean. After the meeting, we flew to Honolulu to visit the Pangs. Richard is a big fisherman, and we stayed our last two nights at their fishing camp outside of Honolulu.

On Saturday, George and Richard went fishing and caught our evening meal. Sunday, our last day in Hawaii, we visited Pearl Harbor and the memorial of the *Arizona*. Hawaii is truly an island of sunshine, palm trees, and flowers of every color.

In 1974, we built a tennis court in our backyard, and in 1978 a swimming pool. Both proved to be assets for our large family, relatives, and friends. Both facilities have been used more each year by our children and now our grandchildren.

My book would not be complete without telling about our three farms, our helpers, and the children's involvement in working on the farms. George wanted our children to have the experience of working on a farm as he did, so we purchased a farm in White House, Tennessee, and hired Abner Frye to be the manager.

Mr. Ab and his wife, Mamie, moved into a house on the farm, and he would oversee the children's work in the summer months. They worked in the tobacco fields and hay fields, and helped with the cows. Before they could drive the thirty miles to the farm, my job was to take Lisa, Laura, Roger, and Kate to the farm every morning, go back home with Nan and Barbara, and drive back to the farm in the afternoon to bring them home. It was a total of 120 miles a day! Nan and Barbara had their time on the farm as they became older. With Mr. Ab's help, the children built a small cabin on our acreage in Hendersonville. It was on the top of the highest hill in Hendersonville, and we enjoyed it as a family until vandals burned it down.

Our farm in Ashland City continues to be a fun spot for family barbecues and dove hunts. Pat and Charles Gruen have been wonderful caretakers and workers with our Hereford cattle. George and I have a small apartment in the barn, with my favorite spot, our screened-in porch with wicker furniture. There is a large room in the barn where we keep medicine and hospital supplies and pack our boxes for Africa. Nurses and doctors at St. Thomas Hospital save supplies for us, and Charlie packs our boxes while Pat labels them.

Over the years, we have had some interesting visitors from other countries. In the 1960s, we entertained Rev. Ithiel Master and Bishop Singh from India.

From Africa, the Swedish Baptist Church sent Rev. Daniel Isai and his daughter, Anita. George had seen Anita in Bosobe and found her to have a congenital heart condition. Dr. Harvey Bender and Dr. Tom Graham found a ventricular septal defect and were unable to operate because of her severe pulmonary hypertension.

From Sweden, we enjoyed a visit from Rev. Sven Ohm, Ingela Eriksson, and the Colldéns, Ollé and Aina. Ingela's husband, Svante, was a doctor with George in Bosobe and died in 1995, possibly from the

Ebola virus. Ollé Colldén was a teacher in the nursing school in Bosobe in the late 1980s.

George asked me one day in the spring of 1990 if a young Chinese doctor, training at St. Thomas Hospital, could live with us for the three summer months, June, July, and August. We had extra bedrooms, so I replied in the affirmative. Dr. Gohui Chang arrived and stayed five months instead of three as planned. Our only real trouble came at mealtime in the evening when we went into the kitchen to fix our different meals. Gohui had the habit of putting rice on to boil and leaving it to watch television. I finally got my point across that he must stay near the stove! Once he marinated some chicken on the counter for three days. When I insisted that he either cook it or put the chicken back in the refrigerator, he cooked it, and before I knew it, George ate a piece. For those five months, there were many Chinese visitors in and out to see Gohui.

In the summer of 1993, George and I went to a mitral valve meeting with our good friends, Marian and Bill Stoney. We made it a special trip, since 1993 was the year of our fortieth wedding anniversary for both couples. Marian and Bill were married in June of 1953 also. We flew to New York, spent the night, and boarded the Concorde for London. Three hours and eighteen minutes later, we landed at Gatwick Airport in England. You only felt the difference when you read how fast we were traveling and how high our altitude was.

In London, we stayed for two days at the Dorchester Hotel, one of the best. We took in some shopping and an evening at the theater, followed by a late supper at the Ritz. The orchestra at the Ritz was playing all the old tunes that the four of us remembered so well.

The next day we boarded a plane for Paris, one of my favorite European cities. George and Bill attended the mitral valve meeting and Marian and I enjoyed the wonderful ladies' extra sightseeing tours of museums and fashion shows.

I must relate an event that took place on our first evening in Paris. We went to a private reception and dinner related to the meeting. The gala event took place in the famous Louvre Museum, home of the Mona Lisa. As I entered the reception room, I noticed a young French boy of about sixteen years entering also. I was puzzled by his presence, but soon forgot

George and Barbara Burrus and Marian and Bill Stoney on the Queen Elizabeth II *on our fortieth anniversary.*

him as I began to talk to others. I was wearing an over-the-shoulder evening bag, and tucked inside was a small pouch that contained my fortieth anniversary present, a diamond pin. Suddenly, I felt my evening bag against my hip and looked down to see my bag opened. I whirled around and caught the young boy by the arm. With his free hand, he handed me the pouch and quickly disappeared. The whole episode took place within minutes, and no one seemed to witness the event. Maybe a little angel was standing at his back to help me detain him. Who knows!

After a week in Paris, we rented a small car and drove toward Chartres, France, where we visited the famous Cathedral of Chartres. The city is built on a hill crowned by the beautiful cathedral.

Our next direction was the Loire Valley of France and visits to the beautiful chateaux and its gardens. We visited Le Chateau d'Amboise, Le Chateau de Chambord, and Le Chateau de Cheverny. My favorite chateau was Le Chateau de Chenonceau because of its gardens and architecture.

Next, we headed toward the port of Cherbourg, France, and our rendezvous with the *Queen Elizabeth II* and our journey home. I mentioned earlier our better accommodations on this trip, and we enjoyed five days of conversation, walks on the decks, and excellent cuisine with the Stoneys, our good friends.

In 1990, George received an honor given by St. Thomas which was recorded in our West End United Methodist Church weekly newspaper.

Burrus Receives Honor

Dr. George R. Burrus, a long time member of West End United Methodist Church, has been named the first recipient of the Saint Thomas Hospital Physician Humanitarian Award.

Burrus, 58, was chosen by his medical colleagues for his service to humanity, loyalty and dedication to Saint Thomas and for demonstrating excellence in the field of medicine. The award was presented at the annual Saint Thomas Medical Staff meeting.

Burrus has been a member of Saint Thomas Hospital's medical staff for 26 years, specializing in thoracic and cardiac surgery.

After completing his medical training, Burrus spent one year in India and two years in Africa as a medical missionary. His relationship to the African mission field has continued as an ongoing effort.

For the past 10 years, Burrus and his wife, Barbara, have returned to Zaire for three to four week mission visits. Originally they filled in for vacationing physicians, but they soon became pivotal in other areas, such as establishing a nursing school.

This nursing school continues to be active as it graduates about 25 African nurses annually. Burrus' current project with the Zaire hospital involves the purchase and installation of an X-ray machine.

Burrus also has set up a foundation in the memory of his daughter, who died early in his medical career. While the foundation was set up to help children, it now aids a variety of medical projects in Africa and in the United States.

Swan, Roger, Bill, and George, "The Burrus Boys."

In April 1993, George's brother, Roger, a doctor of obstetrics and gynecology, became ill with cancer. He lived until September. He was a humanitarian and well liked by his colleagues and friends. George and I missed very few days of his illness and will always remember our visits with "Sonny."

In January 1995, George's older brother, Bill, a retired dentist, came home from Florida and checked into the hospital. The family was stunned to hear that he had cancer, and we lost Bill in the fall of that year. Both Roger's wife, Mary Joyce, and Bill's wife, Emily, were strong and handled the illnesses with inner strength.

The following pages will be my attempt to tell about my five daughters, their educations, occupations, weddings, and children.

Our oldest daughter, Lisa Burrus Turk, was born February 24, 1957, in Nashville, Tennessee. Her birth was frank breech and probably contributed to a dislocated hip. For about eighteen months, she wore a brace and learned to walk in the brace at age thirteen months. Lisa was a happy child, full of curiosity and always on the move. Our experience of my teaching her first-grade work in India was good for both of us since it gave her some attention apart from her siblings.

When we returned to Nashville in 1963, she entered Woodmont Elementary School and was a good student. After Woodmont, she entered West End Junior High School, and her talents for music and drama began to appear. She took piano lessons, and as a seventh grader, she earned the lead in a play that was made up mostly of ninth graders. After her seventh grade year, we left Nashville, and she studied for a few months in a Catholic girls' school in Brussels, Belgium. In Africa, she went to TASOK (The American School of Kinshasa) and once again had the lead in the school play.

She lived in the Disciples of Christ Hostel in Kinshasa and soon became good friends with the Goodall children, Julia and Harry. As I stated earlier, their mother, Eunice, was my friend in Peabody College, and she was killed in a small plane crash in Africa.

In 1971, we returned to Nashville from Africa, and Lisa entered Hillsboro High School. She joined the choral group and enjoyed their activities and concerts.

As a senior, she was given the role of Eliza in *My Fair Lady*. Even if she is my daughter, I have to say she was fantastic. Her voice, stage presence, and expression were very professional. After Lisa married, she was in two plays in Nashville, *Fiddler on the Roof* and *Hello, Dolly*.

After graduating from high school, Lisa entered Vanderbilt University School of Nursing. She lived in the dorm on campus and joined the Kappa Delta sorority. During the winter of her junior year, Lisa was presented at the Tri Delta Eve of Janus Ball, which was a family evening complete with grandmothers and dates.

While at Vanderbilt, Lisa met Alan Mark Turk from Long Island, New York. Alan was getting a degree in law and business at the same time, and he and Lisa decided to marry in August of 1980. Alan was the first of my five wonderful sons-in-law. After Lisa graduated from Vanderbilt, she went to Africa with George and Roger for a month, and on the way home stopped off in England to visit her cousin, Jennye Dale Greene. Jennye's

Lisa, Alan, Jessica, and Ben Turk. Daughter no. 1.

husband, Jeff, was a Rhodes scholar in Oxford, England.

Lisa and Alan married on August 30, 1980. Lisa converted to Judaism, and they were married by Rabbi Falk and our good friend, Rev. Jack Walton. It was a beautiful ceremony by the pool and garden of our home. Lisa's sisters and Roger were in the wedding party, as was Alan's brother, Andrew. We fell in love with his parents, Renee and Fred Turk. Over the years, we have visited them in New York, and they come south often.

Their wedding reception was held at the Belle Meade Mansion in Nashville and was a joyful affair with good food and music. Frances Pilkington's catering service was responsible for the excellent cuisine, and she fixed the food for all five of our weddings. I could always depend on her services being the best.

Lisa and Alan were blessed with two bright children, Jessica Ellen Turk and Benjamin Burrus Turk. Jessica was born on March 28, 1984, and Ben was born on December 19, 1986. They enjoy sports and music activities and like to visit Dear and Papa. Before the first grandchild was born, I decided upon the name Dear for me, since grandchildren choose their own name if it is left up to them and you might not like it. George wanted to be Papa. It is a wonderful way to get your sons-in-law to call you Dear.

Lisa went back to Vanderbilt in August of 1995 to study for her master's degree in Psychiatric Nursing. Lisa has the gift of perception and understanding that is necessary for her field of work.

The following is an unedited letter written by Jessica during her fifth year in school. It really is my life in a nutshell!

2 Jessica Turk
04–27–95
English
2nd Draft

I ADMIRE MY GRANDMOTHER

By Jessica Turk

Barbara Jean Burrus was born in Columbia, TN on July 8th 1931. She was the eldest of three. Barbara's favorite doll was a Shirly Temple which she treasured. As a young girl she attended the Unirvirsty School and later went to college at Peabody.

One day while Barbara was sitting on the front steps of Peabody. My grandfather [George] came and said Hi, from then on they were boyfriend and girlfriend. On June of 1953 they got married. By then George had his doctorate in cardiac surgeon. Barbara had her graduate in teaching.

From the years 1957 to 1968 Barbara home seven letters that said P.S. I'm pregnant. In 1958 Barbara moved to Houston with her first baby, Lisa, my mother. Lisa was born with a dislocated hip but was caught earliy and had to wear a brace for a year. After Lisa was born then Laura was born then Roger, Katie, Ellen, Nan, and Bozi [Barbara]. Ellen was born in India. She was born retarted and died at the age of four in 1968.

When Lisa was in 8th grade in 1969 the Burrus family moved to Belgium. George was in Belgium for nine months to study tropical diseases before he would go to Africa to be a missionary. In Africa the family lived in Zaire, in a little town called Bosobe. There the family lived for two years.

As years pass the children grew up and have children. Lisa became a nurse and is married to a lawery named Alan Turk. They have two children named Ben (8) and Jessica (11). Jessica also had a dislocated hip like her mother. Laura is married to the treasure of some Atlanta company. They have three children named Charlie (8) Caroline (6) and George (1). Laura's husband's name is Charles Smith. Katie is married to Joe Girffen a plastic surgeon. They have three children named Ellen (5) [Emma (4) and Millie (4)] twins. Roger died in the fall of 1992 he had just finished his P.H.D. in Science and had a heart attack at the age of 32. Roger's death shook the family. Barbara remained strong and kept Roger in her heart.

Recently Nan who is married to Tom Cox is pregnant again after she already has Katie (3) and Burrus who is 9 months. Bozi is married to Jim Figie and they just had a daughter Taylor.

Laura Burrus Smith was my second-born child and made her appearance on December 13, 1958. Laura weighed eight pounds and thirteen ounces, and she was my first Texan. She was born at Methodist Hospital in Houston, Texas. When she was ten days old, she took her first airplane ride back to Nashville, Tennessee, for Christmas. She was an easy baby with an even temperament. Even as a child, Laura wanted to tend to her siblings and organize their activities. She was like a mother hen watching over her chicks, a very good mother hen I must say. This trail followed on through her early years, during the work on the farm and later as we traveled to India, Africa, and camping in Europe.

In India, she would divide her time between Lisa's classroom and playing with Roger and Kate in the upstairs playroom. Laura attended Woodmont Elementary School, and when we moved to Brussels, Belgium, she attended the Catholic girls' school with Lisa. When we arrived in Kinshasa, she was ready for the sixth grade, and it was with an anxious heart that I left her in the Methodist Presbyterian Hostel as a boarder to attend the American School of Kinshasa. She adjusted well, and the following are unedited letters that she sent to my mother and Uncle Bob. My mother had remarried five years after my father's death, and we were all very fond of her husband, Bob Hughes. We called him Uncle Bob.

Kinshasa

Dear Mimi and Uncle Bob,

It was so good to hear from you. I just love to hear from my relatives and friends. How are you all doing? I am doing just fine. I had a little sore throat but it is better.

My family left last Tuesday. I do miss them but I don't mind living in the hostel. I am anxious to see what Boshwe is like. They say it is nice.

Our schoolclass have had a couple of tests. We had a Math test, a Science test, and a couple of Spelling tests. I did pretty good on them.

I got new glasses about a week ago. The frames are brown. The lens are the same power. Lisa also got some new ones.

Our elementary school is having a book fair. I am saving my money for it. They are going to cost about 20 macuta (40 cents). They ordered them from the states.

I am taking piano lessons from a lady named Miss Frisen. I think she is a good teacher and she is very nice. I have piano lessons for 30 minutes. Two of my other roomates take lessons too. Well, I guess that's all I have to say. Write soon.

Your grandaughter,

Laura

Dec. 26, 1969
Kinshasa

Dear Mimi and Uncle Bob,

Did you have a Merry Christmas? I had a very nice one. Santa was very nice to me. I got some clothes, an African purse, a cosmetic case, candy, an African figure, some cards, some money, and little odds and ends that went in my stocking. I got a poem book.

I have been home about a week, and I am enjoying it. I have had fun riding the bicycles. We have two. For Christmas Roger got a light to go on one of the bicycles. He likes it very much. We had two Christmas trees and pretty ornaments.

Today we went to a market which was pretty big. A lot of people were there. I will say good-by now. Write soon.

Love,

Laura

Kinshasa

Dear Mimi and Uncle Bob,

How are you all doing? I am doing allright. School is going pretty good. We had a Math Test and I got 74%. Since a lot of us did not do very good we took it over. On the second test I got 94%. I did better. I missed three. On a science test I missed one and I got an A. I thought I did all right on it.

I got new glasses. The frames are brown and square. I like them. Lisa got some new ones and so did Dad. I think Lisa likes her's. I had to get new lens because my others didn't fit.

Edie Jackson, my roomate had a birthday. Sandra, Nancy and I got her a present. We got her some potatos chips and some sour balls. She liked them.

About a week ago there was a square dance at the Baptist hostel. It was so much fun. I squared danced two times. At the end I was very tired. There were refreshments and cokes. We stayed till about 10:00.

Lisa is doing allright. I think she really likes the hostel. She rooms with one girl. There hostel is a lot smaller than mine is.

We have a tennis court here at the hostel. I play with my roomate about once a week. Sometimes we don't even play once a week.

But we have fun playing. For my birthday Dad got me a badmitten set. I also like playing that. There are four rackets, so all of my roomates and I can play together.

How are all the cousin's? I sure do miss them. Well I guess that is all the news I have to say. Write soon. I sure do miss you all.

Your granddaughter,

Laura

May 10, 1970
Kinshasa

Dear Mimi and Uncle Bob,

Thank you so much for the nice letter you sent me. I always enjoy getting mail from my relatives and friends. I have been talking with the family over a radio used here for communication and they said they were all fine. Everyone is busy.

Guess what? I am getting a kitten. Mom and Dad said I could. My roommate's cat had a litter of kittens and she asked me if I wanted one. I said yes. She is leaving for the states and needed to get rid of them. I am very happy.

Not much news has happened since I last wrote you all. Last Thursday since there was no school our hostel went to the caves in Thysville. The caves are much like the ones in Kentucky. They are called the Mamouth Caves. In Thysville there are blind fish. Our hostel parent, Uncle Red, caught one and showed it to us. It does not have a socket for its eyes. It was very interesting. We spent the day going through the caves. At some places it was so low that you had to climb on your hands and knees. Though we came back tired and dirty we had a great time.

This past Saturday we (kids in our hall) painted our hall. It is painted a light blue. I think it is very pretty.

Next week we are going to paint the bathrooms. We will make all different designs on the walls. We think we will put footprints on one of the walls. I think that would be so funny.

I am going to be in a piano recital. I am very scared. My teacher wants me to play two songs. I hope I don't get scared and mess up. I bet I will. Lisa is taking from the same teacher and will probably be in it too. She is using one of my books that Poppi sent me. I like them very much.

Friday night my roommates and I had over two guests to spend the night. We played games while the older kids went to a party. We had alot of fun. After a little while we had delicious ice-cream, and kool-aid. We had a fun night.

Thank you so much for sending my patterns. I have not yet received them yet but I am sure I will get them soon.

I sure hope Granny Judd is feeling better. I hope she is getting well. Tell Granny Judd a big HELLO from me and that I sure do miss her, and also tell Miss D a big HELLO and that I miss her. How is Miss D doing? How are all the relatives. Tell them all hello. I sure do miss all of them.

Well I guess that is all the news. I love you all. Write soon.

Love,

Laura

Laura, Charlie III, Charlie IV, Caroline, and George. Daughter no. 2.

After we returned from Africa, Laura went to West End Junior High and started playing basketball. She was on Hillsboro High's girls' team and was a favorite among her teammates. In high school, Laura was the prom queen, and upon graduation she received the DAR (Daughters of the American Revolution) Citizenship Award for an outstanding senior. During junior and senior high school, Laura took an active part in the youth work at West End United Methodist Church. She was president of the youth group and rarely missed a meeting.

She entered Vanderbilt University and joined the Kappa Delta sorority, becoming president her senior year. Her major was business and economics. She was presented at the Eve of Janus Ball her junior year, and again, we enjoyed the family evening with grandmothers and friends.

After graduation in 1980, Laura moved to Atlanta and entered Georgia State University for her master's degree in marketing and business. While a student, she met Charles Rufus Smith III, a young man from Annandale, Virginia. He had graduated from Georgia Tech and was getting his MBA from Georgia State also.

Laura and Charlie married in May of 1984 at West End United Methodist Church. We had met his parents, Nancy and Rufus, a retired army colonel, the previous spring and enjoyed their company very much. Charlie had three sisters, Carolyn, Dana, and Alison, who were in the wedding and a brother, Greg, one of his groomsmen. We had the reception at home, and my friend and caterer, Frances Pilkington, came through again with a beautiful presentation of excellent food. We tented the tennis court and thus had a large area, plus a ready-made dance floor.

Laura and Charlie settled in Atlanta, Laura working in management with AT&T, and Charlie with Scientific Atlanta. They were blessed with three beautiful children, Charles Rufus Smith IV, born December 5, 1986, Caroline Brasfield Smith, born May 10, 1989, and George Roger Smith, born May 6, 1994.

My third daughter was Kate Brasfield Burrus, born March 27, 1961, in Houston, Texas. From the very first, Kate was a sweet, sensitive little girl who adored her big brother, Roger. When we left for India, Kate was sixteen months old, and as I mentioned earlier, she paced in her baby bed with chicken pox for two weeks. It seemed the safest place for her to be in that one room on the boat, *Circassius*. She loved the ayah, Ruth, in India and spent her days playing with and following Roger. I do believe that she was meant to be with me the early morning of Roger's death and share those first moments of grief.

She attended West End United Methodist Church kindergarten and was so proud to be in a split first grade-second grade class with Roger. She always cooperated within the family unit, whether it was traveling, getting dressed, or working on the farm.

Kate adjusted to her French school experience quite well and really liked to camp in a tent in Europe. When we moved on to Africa and up into Bosobe, she played every day with the Swedish children in our compound and actually began to speak Swedish.

I taught Kate her third-grade work in Bosobe, along with Roger's fourth grade, and she was a joy to teach. When we moved to Kinshasa and lived next to the Roger Youman family, Kate and Joy Youman played every day, skipping rope or playing in an old abandoned car in the backyard. Our Nan and the two Youman boys, John and Roger, would sit in the car for hours and pretend with Kate and Joy.

After we came home from Africa, Kate went to Head Elementary School, Washington School, and West End Junior High School, where she played basketball. Her interest in basketball lasted throughout Hillsboro High School, and she would always give George a stern look when he would yell some moves for her to make on the playing floor. She was very active in the Civinettes, a service club, was an attendant to the football homecoming queen, and enjoyed a social sorority called S.A.P. sorority. Kate's grades were good because she studied and was organized.

Upon graduation from Hillsboro, she entered Vanderbilt University School of Nursing, where she was a member of Kappa Alpha Theta sorority. She also received her master's degree from Vanderbilt in critical care nursing. She worked for Vanderbilt Hospital after graduation in staff development in surgical intensive care. She was presented at the Eve of Janus Ball in 1982 and Bal D'Hiver in 1984.

While working at Vanderbilt, she met a young surgical resident, Dr. Joe Asa Griffin III, from Florence, South Carolina. Joe had rotated through St. Thomas and trained with George's group, operating with George upon occasion. Little did he know that George was his future father-in-law.

Kate went to Zaire, as I have already mentioned, in 1985 and spent a month helping her daddy and using her nursing skills.

Kate and Joe married May 30, 1987, at West End United Methodist Church. It was a large wedding because Joe had three sisters, Jody, Lisa, and Leslie, and Kate had four sisters plus a few friends. The music was especially beautiful, since Joe and a friend who play the organ planned every detail of the music. We liked Allene and Dr. Joe Jr., a dentist in Florence, very much, and they have always made us welcome in

Florence. Allene and Joe both attended Peabody College in Nashville, so we had something in common from the first time we met.

Joe did his plastic surgery residency at Vanderbilt, so for a few years, we had them in Nashville. We missed them when they moved to Florence, but understood that Joe planned to return to Florence to practice plastic surgery. On October 2, 1990, their first child, Barbara Ellen Griffin, was born in Florence, South Carolina. Dear made it about an hour before she was born; however, I was not so lucky for Kate's next delivery. When we returned from Africa in 1991, Kate had news of twins to be born in January of 1992.

The following description of events is from an article written by Jumana Swindler in the *McLeod Magazine*, volume 7, issue 2, 1992:

A PAIR OF MIRACLES

Twice the Struggle
Twice the Blessing

by Jumana A. Swindler

The soft, tenderly designed birth announcements were sent a bit belated, considering that the pair of fragile bundles arrived so early.

On the card, with a pink bow painted at the top, the happy proclamation mailed out in January read:

Kate and Joe joyfully announce the homecoming of their precious twin girls born October 17, 1991

Millie Howard Griffin
2 lbs., 7 oz.
Emma Williams Griffin
2 lbs., 6 oz.
. . . We will call them Millie and Emma.

What has since become a pair of blessings, began with apprehension and fear. For the Griffins, last October introduced the first chapter of a story whose ending was unclear—living happily ever after was then a question of their being able to live at all.

Millie and Emma, somewhat overzealous in their debut in this world, arrived after only 27 weeks. Full term babies are normally born between 36 weeks to 40 weeks, with 38 weeks being the average.

The twins' mother, Kate Griffin, explains that she went into pre-term labor at 22 weeks. "I'd gone to the doctor that day because I was having contractions."

Considering the strong possibility that the babies might be born too early to survive, Kate was admitted to the hospital and placed on quite a few medications to control the labor. Contractions were never completely stopped, however.

A cardio-vascular, critical care nurse herself, Kate knew the seriousness of her situation both as a professional and as a mother. She had paused her nursing career to have Barbara Ellen, the Griffins' only other child, a little more than a year before.

After an uneventful first pregnancy, said Kate, "This time, I was in the labor and delivery section at McLeod for five weeks—but not in full blown labor. I knew I had to be calm and patient. Each day more meant a better chance for my babies to survive."

The doctors and nurses were excellent, she said. "They did the best they could to reassure me and take care of my needs. They were supportive and caring at a very difficult and frightening time in my life. Knowing the high risk involved in my pregnancy, I was comfortable—trusting in the experience of my physicians, Dr. Adams and Dr. Odell, and a very nurturing staff."

Kate said that she had anticipated the babies coming early—but never dreamed that they would try at 22 weeks.

During those weeks in the hospital, Kate received very few visitors and "I concentrated a great deal on keeping relaxed." Then at 27 weeks, the babies came, catching Kate and her husband, Joe, off guard. Joe, a local plastic surgeon, was in California attending a plastic surgery board review when Millie and Emma were born.

Immediately, their care began in the McLeod Neonatal Intensive Care Unit, where premature babies receive the chance for a healthier start.

From the beginning, the NICU doctors gave Kate no false expectations. "They simply did not know how these babies would do," said Kate. "It was all uncertain because they were so very little."

Emma and Millie were born with lung disease—because of their prematurity and underdevelopment at birth. They required ventilation almost initially and soon were given a new drug that allowed them to keep their airways open as well as promote the exchange of gases.

Kate compares the experience of having twins in the NICU to a rollercoaster ride. "We were up one day and down the other. There were some close calls. At one point, their lungs collapsed and required chest tubes. In my mind, I had doubts about whether our beautiful babies were going to live."

What really impressed Kate was the complete honesty of the doctors. They gave hope when there was hope, and kept the Griffins aware of the problem when there was bad news.

"As far as friends and family members, some sent flowers—not baby gifts, when the babies were born. They really didn't know how to respond to us and we didn't know what to expect, either," Kate said.

Emma became very sick when her lung disease worsened. Millie was sick, but stable. Through various treatments, and persistent NICU staff efforts, every day became another step toward better health for both babies. Their improvement was noticeable.

"It is unbelievable what a tiny little body can do—miraculous. They say that premies are fighters; I believe it," said Kate.

The Griffins and their babies were part of the McLeod NICU family for 88 days. "Despite the frustration of what we were going through as parents, we felt safe. Our babies were in great hands . . . and so were we."

The McLeod Neonatal Intensive Care Unit averages a daily census of about 21 babies. The smallest baby to have survived since the NICU started with the new Medical Center in 1979 weighed about 1 pound, 6 ounces.

According to Hart Smith, interim director of the McLeod NICU, "Our unit was the fourth in the state and currently is the only NICU servicing the entire Pee Dee region.

"We have an excellent mortality rate. After about 27 weeks, our babies have a really good chance of survival."

The twins obviously are among the hundreds of survivors who are living proof of that success.

That's not to say that Millie's and Emma's difficulties are over, but medical technology and expertise are definitely on their side.

Recently, Millie and Emma underwent surgery to remedy the underdevelopment of the vessels which feed the retina. As the babies started to grow their eyes were at risk, but the operations prevented the possibility of bleeding or detached retinas.

Dr. Hugh Gaskin, a local ophthalmologist, followed the twins very closely and performed the surgery on their eyes. "We've seen miraculous results," said Kate.

At seven months old and weighing approximately 12 pounds, the twins are already demonstrating certain personality traits. Millie has a temper, Emma appears more subdued. Millie's the healthier one and seems to be more dominant.

"Both are making small milestones. We're just amazed that we have these wonderful babies at home and well," said Kate.

"When I look back on this experience, it's difficult to remember the babies being so ill. But what I do like to recall is the human touch and emotion displayed by the staff at McLeod. As a critical care nurse I know that often you can get into a routine and forget that patients are people. But that never happened in the NICU. Their sensitivity and care gave us confidence and helped us bring home healthier children that may never have even had the chance to come home," added Kate.

"We feel very blessed."

Kate, Joe, Barbara Ellen, Emma, and Millie. Daughter no. 3.

Indeed, the twins were miracles, and I could not believe it when at age four they skied part of the mountain at Snowmass, Colorado. George and I wanted to add our feelings of gratitude to McLeod Hospital in Florence, and we purchased an infant respirator for the McLeod Neonatal Intensive Care Unit. This purchase was made through the Roger-Ellen Burrus Fund, and we felt that it was all a part of "our plan to assure the health of other children in the future."

As I mentioned earlier, Nan Burrus Cox was born when Ellen was two years old. She was born May 17, 1965, in Nashville, Tennessee, and was our fifth daughter. From the very first, Nan liked being a girl, dressing up and playing with her dolls. She was very petite with large brown eyes and a big vocabulary for her age. At age four and one-half months, she sat alone after getting up all on her own. That was a preview of her athletic abilities to come.

When we went to Africa, Nan was four years old, and in Bosobe she found a good friend in a Swedish playmate, Marita Larson. After we moved to Kinshasa, Nan went to kindergarten at TASOK and rode a special bus with Lisa, Laura, Roger, Kate, and the Youman children. She had a very determined personality, a trait that served her well for future events.

After we returned home in 1971, we noticed a small limp in her walk and took her for an examination. She was diagnosed as having Legg-Perthes, a disease of the hip joint. The treatment was to bear no weight on the hip for two years and to sleep in a brace at night. Her leg was held with a sling, and she used crutches. To my knowledge, Nan did not bear weight on that leg for two years due to her determination. It was not easy for her, but she never wavered from our instructions and methods. I was proud of her determination.

When she entered junior high school, we were thankful and amazed to watch her play basketball with obvious talent for the game. She continued to play basketball at Hillsboro High School and was honored her senior year by being elected Most Valuable Player (MVP) in volleyball in the NIL (Nashville Interscholastic League). Also, she was honored in basketball as being all-NIL and on the second team in the state of Tennessee.

I have already mentioned that Nan accompanied George to Nashville from Africa in the spring of 1971 by way of Israel. After George's meeting, they returned to Africa by way of Lambarene, Gabon, site of Albert Schweitzer's hospital.

Nan was an attendant to the homecoming queen during her junior year, and after graduation, she entered Vanderbilt University School of Nursing. She joined Kappa Alpha Theta sorority and was presented at the Eve of Janus Ball and was queen of the Bal D'Hiver, a Theta alumnae event. After graduation from nursing school, Nan worked at Egleston Children's Hospital in Atlanta, Georgia.

At Vanderbilt, Nan met Thomas Fagan Cox from Houston, Texas, and they were married on October 7, 1989, at West End United Methodist Church. Once again, we enjoyed a beautiful evening of commitment, family, friends, gorgeous flowers, and excellent food. We were once again

Nan, Tom, Kate, Burrus, and Elizabeth. Daughter no. 5.

blessed with good in-laws, Ann and Fagan Cox from Houston, Texas. Tom had one sister and two brothers, Shari, Keith, and David. Nan and Tom settled in Houston for a year or so, and Nan worked at Texas Children's Hospital where her father had trained with Dr. Denton Cooley some thirty-two years ago.

Before her marriage, Nan had gone to Zaire with George and me to help out in the hospital, and in 1990, Nan and Tom joined us for another trip back to the jungle.

They were blessed with three lovely children, Kate McAllister Cox born July 16, 1992, Thomas Burrus Cox born October 27, 1994, and Elizabeth Fagan Cox born November 10, 1995.

When I was in the delivery room with my seventh child, I remember hearing my brother-in-law, Roger, say, "The prettiest one you've got!" I knew then that we had our sixth little girl, Barbara Burrus, born

Barbara, Jim, and Barbara Taylor. Daughter no 6.

September 4, 1968, in Nashville, Tennessee. From the very first, Barbara was a blonde with blue eyes. At the very young age of nine months, she was carried to Europe and Africa by her family, and she camped all over Europe. Of course, Barbara does not remember the events; however, she saw pictures and heard stories from her siblings. When we camped, the first thing that we did was set up the playpen, and Barbara would watch the other children help set up camp. She took her first steps in Stockholm, Sweden, and then on to Africa for two years.

In Bosobe, we had a young African girl of sixteen who helped with Barbara while I was teaching Nan, Kate, and Roger. Esther, the helper, nicknamed Barbara "Bozi," and it stuck. She was known as Bozi through school and even after she married.

Barbara started kindergarten at Woodmont Elementary School and attended Head Middle School, West End Junior High, and Hillsboro

Giving away Nan with one more to go.

Barbara and her five daughters—Lisa, Nan, Barbara, Barbara Jr., Kate, and Laura.

Our last wedding, and so beautiful!

Eleven of the grandchildren, minus Charlie.

High School where she played volleyball and basketball.

When the time came to choose a college, she surprised everyone by not choosing Vanderbilt as the other five children had done. Instead, she headed west and the University of Colorado. She was a good skier, and perhaps this was part of her plan. She graduated with a B.S. degree in psychology and a certification in elementary education. She planned to be a teacher for elementary-age children like her mother did some forty years earlier. She was a member of the Kappa Kappa Gamma sorority at Colorado, and after graduation she was presented at the Eve of Janus Ball in Nashville.

In 1988, Barbara returned to Africa with George and me, and she renewed her friendship with Esther, her nurse and nanny for two years.

Barbara chose the University of Virginia to pursue her master's degree, and she completed her work in educational curriculum and instruction. Then it was back to Boulder, Colorado, to teach for a few years. She had met a young man, James Kahl Figge, while she was at the

University of Colorado, and they married in Nashville, Tennessee, on August 7, 1993. They moved to Sun Valley, Idaho, where Barbara continued to teach, ski, bike ride, and jog while Jim started a real estate career. Her jogging and running were in expectation of a twenty-six-mile marathon later.

We could not leave out Charlie Smith IV.

On July 15, 1995, they were blessed with the birth of Barbara Taylor Figge, my eleventh grandchild. Jim grew up in Kansas City, Kansas, and we have enjoyed knowing his mother, Joanne, father, Jim, and stepmother, Sandy. He was the oldest of four boys, Chris, Peter, and Stephen.

Even though she was the youngest child of seven, I must say that Barbara never seemed spoiled or demanding. She has always been very independent and resilient.

In the spring of 1996, Barbara ran a marathon in Coeur d'Alene, Idaho. She ran the 26.2 miles in 3 hours and 39 minutes. George and I flew out to cheer her on and to keep Barbara Taylor while Mama ran the race. She had been in training for almost a year, and she realized her dream. However, she was not interested when George said that the Boston Marathon was next! We enjoyed staying in Spokane, Washington, before the race and viewing beautiful Hayden Lake in Coeur d'Alene, Idaho, for breakfast with friends between the start and finish lines. Barbara came in third in her age group. There were about one thousand people in the total marathon.

Our five girls have always been and continue to be God's greatest gifts to George and me. They have supported us in so many ways, for which I am so grateful.

CHAPTER 7

Tragic Changes—1992

In October of 1992, my life changed forever in one second of news that my only son, Roger, was dead. The finality of it still overwhelms me from time to time, and I will never be the same. Somehow, Ellen's death was a release for her and her quality of life, while Roger was young and had so much left to give to his research.

I chose this time to write about my only son, Roger, since I am in Snowmass, Colorado, surrounded by George, four daughters, their husbands, and ten of my twelve grandchildren. Such a happy reunion can only support my thoughts as I look back on his life.

George Roger Burrus was born March 22, 1960, at Hermann Hospital in Houston, Texas. He weighed in at eight pounds and was the third child for George and me. His two older sisters, Lisa and Laura, were excited about their baby brother.

As a child, Roger was even-tempered and played well with his peers. He joined the Boy Scouts and always wanted to apply what he learned when we went on family camping trips. One summer, he went to Boy Scout camp and won the Good Citizenship Award. He spent his early elementary years at Woodmont Elementary School in Nashville with the exception of our two years in Africa. I taught Roger his fourth-grade work, and he spent his fifth grade in the American School of Kinshasa in Zaire.

Roger's early soccer training was the result of many games in the jungle with the African boys, excellent soccer players themselves. Roger had an ear for languages and quickly picked up the native language of Zaire, Lingala, and some French. When the African people would come to our door to sell eggs or vegetables, I would summon Roger to talk for me. He wrote this letter from Africa to my mother and Bob, her husband.

Dear Mimi and Uncle Bob,

I am in Kinshasa. I enjoy Boshwe. It is very cool and pretty. Please come here. If you don't you will not see my monkey and I will be upset. The stamps on my letter please send back. I killed a viper. Very dangerous.

Love,

Roger

When we returned home from Africa in 1971, Roger entered Head Elementary School in Nashville and was president of the chess club.

During the following summer, Roger took a test for Montgomery Bell Academy. MBA is an excellent school for boys, grades seven through twelve. Our girls went to public school and did well, but we felt Roger needed male companions since he lived with six sisters.

His strong points at MBA were French, tennis, and soccer. He was on the first tennis team as a freshman and held his place for four years.

During Roger's junior year at MBA, George and Roger got permission from Mr. Carter, the headmaster, to go to the U.S. Open Tennis Tournament in Forest Hills, New York. They watched the Jimmy Conners—Bjorn Borg match, which they said was great.

Roger took the national French test and placed first for the southern states for two years. He played football, and as a freshman was injured. He broke a leg and was in the hospital for a month and in bed at home for two months. He was eager to keep up with his studies, and the teachers from MBA would come by to tutor him.

Roger was a good steady skier and enjoyed our condo in Snowmass, Colorado. He enjoyed skiing with friends, Elena and Brent Campbell and Mary and Andy Brennan.

During his senior year at MBA, the soccer team went to the state championship in Chattanooga, Tennessee. The game ended in a 0–0 tie with Roger having a free penalty kick. He kicked a banana shot high into the corner of the goal for the big win! His team won the state championship, and Roger was elected Most Valuable Player of the game. After the game, George took the team to the Chattanooga Choo-Choo for dinner.

Roger was accepted at the University of North Carolina, University of Virginia, and Vanderbilt University. He chose the University of Virginia and spent his freshman year there. Much to our delight, he transferred to Vanderbilt for his undergraduate work and master's work in molecular biology. His work for his doctorate degree in pathology took longer than usual because halfway through he questioned some earlier data and would not build upon the data. He proved it to be somewhat questionable and had to start over on another project. His intense integrity would not allow him to look the other way and publish untrue statistics. He received his Ph.D. in pathology in December of 1991. His work was accepted in the Medical Library at Vanderbilt.

Roger was not one for pretense or only being friendly with the one on top; he was sincerely honest and a friend to people in every station of life. In August of 1991, he moved to Boulder, Colorado, and took a job in Denver, Colorado, at the Eleanor Roosevelt Institute for cancer research.

One evening in October of 1992, George had gone to the hospital for an emergency operation. My daughter, Kate Griffin, was at home with me that night. We had had a family reunion the preceding weekend when Katie Cox was christened, and I was driving home to Florence, South Carolina, with Kate and her girls later that week. About two-thirty on that morning of October 27, 1992, the phone rang. I answered it and a voice said, "Is this the home of Dr. George Burrus?" I replied, "Yes. This is Mrs. Burrus speaking." The voice in the emergency room said, "Mrs. Burrus, your son, Roger, is dying, dying. He is dead."

At first, I hoped that it was a bad dream and I would wake up to find everything all right. That was not the case, and a part of me was changed forever. I woke up Kate and she helped to contact Barbara's boyfriend, Jim Figge, who lived in Boulder. He went over to Barbara's apartment and told her about Roger. They would handle things from that end.

My next thought was George. For the second time, our friend, Bill Stoney, came to our aid—once when he operated on George in 1983 for heart surgery and now to go to the hospital and tell him about his son's death. Roger's autopsy showed death from a heart attack, having had two previous ones, evident from the autopsy. I am sure that Roger thought any previous pain was only indigestion. He was only thirty-two when he died and enjoying his work at the institute.

Family and friends gathered at the gravesite at Spring Hill Cemetery, and we laid him to rest beside his sister, Ellen. Our five daughters, their husbands, and eight grandchildren were a source of real comfort to George and me. We added Roger's name to our Ellen Burrus Fund, which enables us to help other people in Africa and America with health problems.

The following quotations have sustained me during periods of heartbreak and intense grief:

> Why do the people who we love and need so much have to leave? They do not all the way. You still have them inside, and you can't lose them from there.
>
> —Nora Roberts

> The soul would have no rainbow, if the eyes had no tears.
>
> —Author Unknown

> Give sorrow words. The grief that does not speak knits up the o'er-wrought heart and bids it break.
>
> —William Shakespeare

> For us there is no farewell. Only a momentary parting.
>
> —Kathryn Lynn Davis

The following tribute to Roger was written by Elena and Dr. Brent Campbell, two close friends who brought George and me a ski picture of Roger with the following words:

With Roger, there were words left . . .
The movie he was writing
The promise to some day ski the wall
The chance to say "I love you"
Our children, he will not know.

To hide his incredible sensitivity, Roger
would have denied us this tragedy, but
would admit the mean irony in the
distortion of life's 'Natural History:'
Parents are not to bury their children.

We remember Roger:
Red rough knees poking through
an overworked raincoat.
The disheveled hair and glasses midway
down the bridge of his nose,
our beloved scientist.
His direct gaze and relentless inquisitiveness,
and his occasionally painfully
straight forward truthfulness.
His offbeat sense of humor and quick,
disarming smile. The gracious
countenance borrowed from his father.
A golden-haired soccer player with
shifty, sure footed moves. The games
of poker in his mother's warm kitchen.

We love Roger deeply and miss him terribly.
Yet somehow, we know that he is at peace.
All is well with our precious friend.

We received the following letter from the Eleanor Roosevelt Institute (ERI) for cancer research, which meant so much to our family:

Eleanor Roosevelt Institute
October 28, 1992

Dear Dr. & Mrs. Burrus:

All on the staff here at Eleanor Roosevelt Institute will miss a very important and special scientist—George Roger Burrus.

Yesterday afternoon, Dr. Clarence Snelling of Iliff School of Theology, conducted a memorial service here at the institute. It was a time for us to mourn Rog's death but also to celebrate his life. Dr. Snelling urges us "to continue the important work being done at this community of research." He suggested that this will be our way to pay the highest tribute to Rog.

Dr. Michael Sinensky, in whose laboratory Rog worked, noted that, "Rog brought to his work a level of idealism; he cared deeply for his research. He took great joy in his work. Rog took research as a calling."

On behalf of all at ERI, I send you and your family my deepest sympathy.

Most sincerely,

David Patterson, Ph.D.
President and Senior Fellow

The following letter from Montgomery Bell Academy was received by our family after establishing the George Roger Burrus Award in 1995:

Dear Dr. and Mrs. Burrus:

Last week's Honors Convocation at MBA was especially meaningful, as it showcased highly deserved recognition for students and for distinguished alumni and friends. The newly created "George Roger Burrus Award," which Lisa and Nan were here to inaugurate, was particularly special.

Thank you, on behalf of our students and faculty, to you and your family for establishing this award. Roger (whom many faculty members present last night remember well, and with fondness) would undoubtedly be pleased. Chris Kellam, the eighth grader selected as this year's recipient, is himself extremely grateful for the $2,000 gift toward the financial aid assistance which accompanies his recognition.

I know you would enjoy Chris. He lives with his parents in Mt. Juliet, started at MBA as a seventh grader, and is described by our faculty as an "All-American Boy." Here are some comments about him: "Bright, handsome, strong character, a quiet leader, highly respected by his peers, solid, dependable, responsible, well-organized, and a nationally ranked swimmer (instantly o.k. with Roger, I imagine)." His grades are consistently in the B+ range, one measure of the wisdom of financial aid which enables him to attend MBA.

The George Roger Burrus Award and $2,000 annually which accompanies it will follow Chris (with review each year) until he graduates from MBA. At that time, we understand that you and your family will assess the award, with your expectation that it will revert to and follow another eighth grade student through graduation at MBA.

Thank you for this tribute to Roger. It is doubly special to MBA, as a student on need-based financial aid becomes the beneficiary of your remembrance of him, as well. All of those who taught and coached Roger here are very pleased by it.

Sincerely,

Thomas S. Weaver Jr.

Our son, George Roger Burrus, 1960–1992.

The following letter was received by Lisa and Alan Turk from the young boy, Christopher Wade Kellam:

Dear Mr. and Mrs. Alan M. Turk,

I am deeply honored to have received such a wonderful award. I have heard many great things about George Roger Burrus, such as being MVP his senior year in soccer.

I myself am a swimmer. I also like biking, running, basketball, and soccer. In swimming I am ranked nationally in my age group. I enjoy it very much.

I also like MBA. As you know, I just finished my 7th grade year, and did very well. My favorite subject this past year has been physical science.

Again I would like to say how deeply honored I am to have received such a prestigious award. Thank you very much.

Sincerely,

Christopher Wade Kellam

June 13, 1995

The following words were spoken at the Honors Convocation at MBA when the award was presented:

Dr. George Roger Burrus was a promising cancer researcher when a heart attack befell him at the premature age of 32. He graduated from MBA in 1978 and counted those years as the most

My mother and sisters, Edwyna and Gayle. Their support was always there.

> formative of his scholastic life. He excelled at MBA as a student-athlete, on the soccer field and in the classroom.
>
> This award is offered in his memory by his parents, Dr. and Mrs. George R. Burrus, and his five loving sisters.

As a family, we have missed and thought about him each day. While thinking about him one day, I realized that my great-grandmother, Laura, lost her only son, my grandfather; that my grandmother lost her only son, my father; and now the third generation experiences this loss of an only son.

CHAPTER 8

Bosobe, Zaire
Africa, 1993–1994

Since there had been some trouble between the military and the people in the country of Zaire during 1992, we were unable to land in Kinshasa in February 1993. Instead, we planned to land in Brazzaville, a city across the Congo River from Kinshasa. Our Missionary Aviation Fellowship (MAF) pilot, Dave French, met us, and we spent the night with his family, Jan, his wife, and Christina and Jonathan, his children.

The next morning we listened over the MAF radio asking us to stop in Semendua on our way to Bosobe. Dave was flying us over the river to Kinshasa for a check of our visas and passports, and on up-country to Bosobe. Our plane did land in Semendua, and we soon noticed that our boxes of medicine were being unloaded from the plane. We were told that it was dangerous for us to go on to Bosobe to help the people. We later learned that the alleged danger was a ploy by the folks in Semendua to prevent us from helping the hospital in Bosobe. The internal conflict between the church in Semendua and the church in Bosobe was such that we were on the outside looking into a "family" conflict. It was easy for us to surmise that the conflict was probably related to finances. There we were, stranded in the village of Semendua, the site of our first night in the interior back in 1969. We went to bed that night with many questions and doubts about our next move. As the sun arose the next morning, George said that maybe we could be of some aid to the Baptist Hospital in Vanga, an hour away by plane from Semendua. We called by radio, and they said, "Come on down. We need you in the operating room today."

God does work in mysterious ways, and the following are some notes I wrote during our stay in Vanga:

> Here I sit by the river, Kwilu, in deep, dark Africa. Since we were unable to go into Bosobe on this trip, we brought the medicine to Vanga, a Baptist mission located on the river Kwilu.
>
> We were welcomed for a week by Dr. and Mrs. Dan Fountain, friends of twenty years. Their cottage is situated high above the river with a spectacular view of the jungle's edge and boats or pirogues on the river. In some ways, I shall miss this river. During the week, I have sat by its side, thinking, wondering, and trying hard to heal. I will always miss my little boy, but I know he is with God. I hope to see him someday. Who knows?
>
> I do not really understand this trip. We came to Africa with twenty-four 70-pound boxes for the people of Bosobe. Because of an unsettled situation, we were kept from reaching our destination. Instead, we went to Vanga. Here, we found a need not unlike Bosobe or any of Africa. During this week, I visited a primary school of K-3 for the children of the African doctors, nurses, and hospital workers. I observed their French and writing classes and saw many bright eyes for Africa's future. The next day Muriam Fountain told me about a contribution she was making to this school in Roger's memory. Don't ever underestimate the good that can come from a chain of events founded in God's love and world.

George received the following note from Leonard Wolcott, a former professor of missions at Scarritt College in Nashville. We had studied under him before going to India in 1962.

Dear George Burrus:

One day I was walking along a hot dusty road in India. There came strongly to my mind an awareness of the people who were keeping me in their prayers.

Again, more recently, on my way to Zaire while in Europe, I sensed the support I was receiving in people's prayers.

Although your trips to Africa are frequent and brief, I want you to know that my prayers are with you and Barbara.

May your trips of mercy be a benefit to many and a joy to you.

Sincerely,

Leonard Wolcott

(Wish I were going along—and could stay there another year.)

The next journey to Bosobe was planned for July 15, 1994. Charlie Gruen had worked long and hard at the farm getting twenty-six, seventy-pound boxes packed. Lisa spent the night of the fourteenth with us in order to take us to the airport early. I suspect that she and George felt that I needed moral support to leave the next day. After our being unable to enter Bosobe the preceding year, my feelings were very unsure about our safety on this trip. Tom Cox, Nan's husband, helped Charlie at the airport, and we were on our way. I looked forward to one night at the Wolfsprung on the way over to Africa.

During the trip from Zurich to Kinshasa, I became restless and unable to sleep. I realized that it was necessary for me to direct my mind to matters other than Africa and the fact that I was thirty thousand feet above the vast Sahara Desert.

While sitting there on the plane, I wondered if I might check out the duty-free shopping aboard. I inquired about some Hermés bracelets, and the stewardess said that they had one or two on board. I asked to see them; however, I needed to have my glasses. I went back to my seat and could not find them, so I spent a good thirty minutes visiting each bathroom on board as it became vacant and looking for my glasses. By then, it was midnight, and I bought my bracelet thirty thousand feet above the Sahara Desert. So much for getting my mind off the present situation!

We arrived in Kinshasa by Swissair and were met by old friends ready to assist our two-week journey. We had made arrangements from the U.S. with MAF to fly us into Bosobe on Wednesday, July 20. Even after we arrived in Kinshasa, MAF reaffirmed the flight, and we only had two days to wait.

The next morning, much to our delight, Dr. Julia Goodall Weeks ran into the guest house at the Methodist Presbyterian Hostel, eager to see Aunt Barbara and Uncle George. My daughter, Laura, lived in this hostel as a sixth grader in 1969, and it brought back good memories of her days there while attending the American School of Kinshasa.

We had arrived on Sunday evening, and on Monday evening, we were invited to dinner with Rev. and Mrs. Ben Hobgood and Julia and Steve Weeks. Every time that I encountered one of Eunice's children, it was with deep emotion and fond memories of my Peabody College friend.

Tuesday morning passed in a meeting with Bosobe friends who had met us at the plane, and we discussed trivial questions of buying some flour, sugar, and rice for up-country. Then, Tuesday afternoon a phone call came from MAF headquarters saying the plane would not be able to take us up-country on Wednesday morning as planned.

After much talking and negotiations with African authorities, we finally were cleared to take the Caravan from Kinshasa to Bosobe direct, with our 1,820 pounds of medicine from St. Thomas Hospital to Bosobe, Zaire, Africa. You cannot conceive of that distance unless you make the journey. I tried to keep my mind off the travel by counting the trips—1969, 1985, 1986, 1987, 1988, 1989, 1990, 1991, 1992, 1993, and 1994. It seemed unreal that I would be called upon, persuaded or whatever, to go that distance to help my fellow human beings. Again, I asked, "Why?" There must be a reason. There is a reason. Maybe my angels know! In my human way, I cannot understand it! I still say, however, that I understood George's compassion, sincere interest, and love in God's healing of humankind through one of His servants. It was George's

How many times would we load up and fly into our small village in Zaire?

compelling drive, not my feelings, that took us back and forth to these people in so much need and yet so far away.

This is as good a time as any to applaud the service of the pilots of MAF headquartered in Redlands, California. These young men and their families come out to serve, take risks, and help other families go in and out of the Bush! This morning before takeoff, the young pilot showed me a picture of his family, and then we prayed for our journey. The following expresses some thoughts that I jotted down during this 1994 visit:

July 25, 1994

Once again, I sit on the banks of the Lukenie River watching the activity of this small village close to Bosobe. George has gone out in a pirogue seated in a chair with tall African men guiding the boat, standing not sitting. I always marvel at how far away I am from Nashville, yet God's people with our same hurts, delights, love, family, and strong desire for survival abound here. Once again, the river calms and heals a part of me. I am sitting on a large trunk of a tree that spreads out over the water, and the limbs are full of little children, probably seeing a white person for the first time. If I could sketch or paint, what a picture I would have. It will have to be etched in my mind for years to come!

The following article was published in December of 1994 in the St. Thomas paper, *Today*, and gives a good summary of our work in Zaire:

Blessings from Out of Africa

Saint Thomas surgeon shares his medical expertise in Zaire

Most Americans would agree that the U.S. offers the finest medical care in the world, but few of us stop to think about what that really means. It is only when we catch a glimpse of some other way of life in some out-of-the-way place that we realize our own good fortune.

Just ask George Burrus, M.D., division head of cardiothoracic surgery at Saint Thomas. Each year for a few weeks, Dr. Burrus donates his time and talents to a small village hospital on a river delta in the central African country of Zaire. Through this medical mission effort, Dr. Burrus has first-hand knowledge of the gulf separating American medical care from that of Third World nations.

The hospital in the village of Bosobe is part of a Baptist mission effort in the region, a remote equatorial area 200 miles from Kinshasa, the country's capital and nearest major city. Although the hospital is regularly staffed by nurses, doctors are in short supply. The past July when Dr. Burrus arrived for a two-week visit, he found there was no other doctor.

For the duration of his stay, Dr. Burrus saw patients with a variety of ailments. There was sleeping sickness, typhoid, leprosy, tuberculosis, complications of childbirth, and what was probably AIDS, although AIDS tests are not readily available locally.

Working conditions at the Bosobe hospital would be considered primitive by U.S. standards, Dr. Burrus said. For example, instruments are sterilized in an old Army-issue sterilizer heated by a kerosene lamp. The hospital accepts patients with infections, because there are so many who need medical help, and because hospital-acquired infections are common anyway. "Things may not be absolutely sterile, but we do the best we can," Dr. Burrus noted.

Electrical power is not always a sure thing in Bosobe. "We bought an X-ray machine from Siemens. When they came to install it, they plugged it in and it started smoking. Now we're working to get the generator corrected so there's enough current," Dr. Burrus said. Until that is completed, the equipment sits idle.

Supplies and medicines are hard to come by. Saint Thomas donates some unneeded surgical supplies, and Dr. Burrus has set up a foundation that helps fund the purchase of medicines. "I'm very thankful to Saint Thomas for making the supplies available," he said. "It might seem a small thing to take instruments, sutures, bandages, and Foley catheters that they were going to throw away, but it's really a big help."

The Bosobe mission began in the 1920's and grew to include a church, a school, and a hospital. It closed in 1957 and remained that way until 1969, when it was reopened by Baptist missionaries from Sweden. Dr. Burrus first went to Zaire with his family in 1969 and lived at Bosobe for two years while the hospital was re-established. Since then, he and his wife, Barbara, have returned there every year for a two to four-week mission visit. They have learned French, the official language of Zaire, and Lingala, a native tongue.

Although medical conditions in Bosobe seem archaic by American standards, the hospital actually has come a long way from even humbler beginnings. "We were able to get the people and funds needed to build an airstrip, for example," Dr. Burrus

A dedicated doctor for sure!

said. This enabled the doctors at Bosobe to get supplies in and patients out to a larger medical facility when needed. It was a great accomplishment, because during the rainy season the dirt roads in and out of Bosobe turn to mud and become almost impassable.

Almost five years ago, Dr. Burrus helped establish a nursing school in Bosobe. Its graduates receive training roughly equivalent to that of an American Licensed Practical Nurse (LPN). "This year while we were there, they dedicated a 'superior institute' to give a graduate nursing degree, sort of like our Registered Nurse diploma," he said.

Steps also have been taken to curb infant mortality. There is a maternity/well baby clinic now, and children receive polio and smallpox vaccinations. In this poor, agrarian society, however, many women have a child every year. Newborns get mother's milk, but the older children often are malnourished.

In the remote region in and around Bosobe, people live in extreme poverty. Few have electricity or transportation. There is little hard currency. The people must grow most of their own food. They raise chickens, pigs and goats and catch fish from the rivers. The mission provides basic services such as education and medical care, in addition to spiritual support.

Dr. Burrus began his own medical mission work in 1962, as part of a Methodist mission to India. His father, Dr. Roger Burrus, was a family physician and surgeon in the Nashville area. The elder Burrus' medical partner, Dr. Dan Mumpower, had been a missionary to Zaire (then known as Belgian Congo) in the 1920's. Dr. Burrus credits his father's associate as an influence on his career decisions.

"I wanted to be a doctor in a place where they didn't have one or where my skills could be used," he said.

In 1990, Dr. Burrus was named the first recipient of the Physician Humanitarian Award now given annually by Saint Thomas. He humbly shrugs off the recognition and admiration of others. "You just try to do the best you can for the most folks with what you've got."

Mimi Ferrell

(Published in *Today*, November/December 1994.)

CHAPTER 9

Bosobe, Zaire

Africa, 1995

Each time we travel, I say, "This was the best." We left Nashville on June 23, 1995, had our usual day in Atlanta, and flew by Swissair on to Zurich. We picked up a small car and drove on to Paris, France. For four years, we have attended Le Club Mitrale in Paris. It is a mitral valve meeting sponsored by Promedica International, and it is an opportunity for the doctors who attend to observe the operating of Dr. Alain Carpentier, world renowned for mitral valve surgery. The women's program is fantastic, and the following is an example of 1995's meeting for the ladies:

YOUR PROGRAM

Saturday 24	Arrival in Paris of Le Club Mitrale Pick up by limo at airport and transfer to hotel Louvre-Concorde.
Evening 7:30 p.m.	Get Together, Welcome cocktail at hotel Salon Rohan—street floor (casual)

Sunday 25	Day at leisure for Club Members. Assistance desk in the lobby for suggestions.
6:30 p.m.	Departure to the Louvre Museum and private visit of the Medieval Fortress. Guides—Louise Aujay & Isabelle Villaud
Dinner 8:00 p.m.	Restaurant "Le Grand Louvre" under the glass pyramid.
Monday 26	Professional program for physicians at hospital American breakfast at restaurant, from 6:30 to 10:00 a.m. Bus leaves hotel at 7:45 a.m.
	Ladies Program/ Discover Paris
	9 a.m. Departure from lobby for a sightseeing tour. Major and most famous Paris landmarks—Visit of the Garnier Opera House and costumes exhibition. Lunch
	Continuation of sightseeing and visit of the "Sainte Chapelle"—Ile de la Cité—Famous 13th c. stained glass windows.
Evening	Free at leisure—Reservation at selected restaurants can be made through the Concierge.
Tuesday 27	Professional program for physicians at hospital Bus leaves hotel at 7:45 a.m.
	9 a.m. Ladies Program Visit of the D'Orsay Museum with Louise Aujay Lunch at "Le Telegraphe" (by noon) 41 rue de Lille #40 15 06 75.

3 to 5:30 Cooking demonstration at the Ritz
Escoffier School of Cuisine.
Entrance rue Cambon near Place
Vendome.

Dinner At restaurant "Le Boeuf sur le toit"
7:30 p.m. Bus transfer from lobby.

Wednesday 28 Professional program for physicians at hospital
Bus leaves at 7:45 a.m.

8:45 a.m Ladies Program
Departure to Giverny located 1 hour from
Paris, located on the Seine River Valley.
Visit of Claude Monet's house.
Lunch at Giverny
Aft. Stop at the Marmottan Museum to see
the waterlilies paintings by Monet. Tea
and pastries in a "Salon de thé" or last
minute shopping, at your convenience.
Closing dinner at Pavillon Le Doyen
Champs Elysées Avenue. (dressy)
7:45 p.m. Departure by bus.

Your limo pick-up time for departure will be given to you in the bus.

Thursday 29 Departure day
Limos provided for transportation to airport or
train station.

My favorite one of the outings was the visit to Claude Monet's house in Giverny, France. After his paintings came his flowers, and his garden is a sight to behold. Several times, I stood on the bridge looking out over the lily pond, both subjects of famous Impressionist art. We viewed the work of many impressionists at the D'Orsay Museum in Paris. I jotted down the following words during my 1995 visit:

> Giverny: I need to rest along the way of Monet's garden in Giverny, France, and marvel at the flowers and famous lily pond I have just witnessed. It truly must be a bit of Heaven on earth! Every flower and every color known to man are a living tapestry to Monet's memory. The quiet flowing stream full of beautiful waterlilies makes me want to pause, sit down on the welcoming bench, and just meditate.

After the meeting in Paris, we headed for Amsterdam to investigate a company named IDA (International Dispensary Association). We talked to them about some medicine for Bosobe, Zaire, and then drove on to Switzerland for two nights at the Wolfsprung. Remon Beffa greeted us and made us welcome at his chalet once again. It was our tenth or eleventh stay with him since 1985 when Kate discovered this beautiful place. We went to Lucerne the next day for a visit with Franz Jolidon, our Swiss Bank representative. He treated us to a lovely lunch in one of the grand old hotels in Lucerne. After the second night at the Wolfsprung, we drove to Zurich and caught a plane for Kinshasa, Zaire.

Some people spend their sixty-fourth birthday rocking, others go out on the town with family or friends, while my birthday was spent flying into the jungle of Africa. Will wonders never cease! We made the trip on a larger plane called the "Caravan." My birthday present was a new bicycle for village transportation. We will leave the bikes with friends and have them for future trips.

Before our takeoff from Kinshasa, the pilot gave a prayer for a safe journey and for the work in Bosobe. As we flew away from Kinshasa over the Congo River, we could see the ferries crossing with hundreds of people, and an occasional pirogue with one lone fisherman. Our journey only took one and one-half hours because of the size of the plane. When we landed, the usual crowd of friends and other people were not present. Communication had failed, and no one was expecting us. They termed it a "surprise" and said that the good doctor had fallen out of the sky!

We quickly settled into "our" house (the same as twenty-six years ago) and began the work ahead. I cautioned George about the use of gloves in his work at the hospital. The outbreak of the Ebola virus gave us some concern, and we decided to double our efforts with cleanliness in the jungle. We felt safe with Jacob as our cook because we could trust him to boil our water and prepare our food in a hygienic way.

After the Swedish missionaries left Bosobe and discontinued their work in that area, we had to plan and bring our own food. We settled for a diet of rice, dried soup, papaya, bananas, peanut butter, instant coffee, cheese, and some local vegetables. Fish was abundant, and sometimes Jacob prepared chicken for George.

We stayed for two weeks because George wanted to be there for two Sundays. Two of the days he spent at small clinics down the river, and the others were spent operating and teaching.

Finally, the day came for our departure. Once again as we flew away from Bosobe, I wondered if it was our last visit. Maybe it's because I'm getting older, but more and more, I wait for God's plan to continue or be a memory for my old age. After all, not many people have had the opportunities that have come my way, living and working with God's children all over the world.

Our pilot this trip was Ron Wismer who asked us about a friend of his in Nashville. She turned out to be a basketball friend of my daughter, Kate. She was Debbie Sherman before her marriage. It is a small world, after all!

We stopped for fuel in Semendua, and one of the workers tried to collect an airplane strip tax from George. He claimed that we owed it coming from Bosobe. George said no tax was needed, since he had the strip built and paid for twenty-six years ago.

We landed in Kinshasa about four o'clock, and George just had to stop by the Ivory Market. He bought some malachite animals to add to our collection.

Before dinner, he met with four medical students whom we are helping in Kinshasa. We hope that they will eventually go back to Bosobe, their village, to work.

After dinner at MPH (Methodist Presbyterian Hostel), George went over to Dr. Julia Goodall Weeks's house to see Julia on some business concerning an African girl that we sent to South Africa for an eye treatment or transplant. While he was there, they called Barbara, my youngest daughter, to find out about her baby due the twenty-fifth of July.

Barbara Taylor Figge, our seventh granddaughter, was born July 15, 1995. She weighed six pounds, six ounces, and was twenty-one inches long. Lisa flew out to Sun Valley to help her for a week. We hope to see her soon, and I know that she will excuse Dear and Papa for being in Africa during such a special occasion as her birth.

The next morning, we got up about five o'clock to board Swissair for the flight to Zurich. We spent the night again in Brunnen. However, our friend of ten years, Remon Beffa, did not have room for one night. Instead, he took us to his parents' home about six miles away from the Wolfsprung. His parents lived in a two-hundred-year-old Swiss chalet. From a castle in Scotland in May to an old Swiss chalet in July!

Remon's mother was of Italian heritage, and her home was full of lovely painted furniture and antiques. She opened the door for me to see her treasure room, and I must say, it took me a few moments to take it all into focus. It was an enchanting child's haven of about five hundred dolls, some one hundred years old, and about two thousand pieces of every small dollhouse furniture and dishes known to man. Tea tables were set for some of the dolls, and stuffed animals, doll buggies, and accessories filled the room. She also tatted lace and showed me some of her lovely work.

We were a little late in leaving for Zurich, an hour away, but caught our plane for home in time. We had been gone for one month, and my thoughts turned to seeing our family and friends.

The following letter is an answer to my request from a young African boy who speaks excellent English and always translates some for us in Africa:

> For your question of inquiry about African black men's belief on white men—
>
> The belief according to which white people are black people who died some time ago is heard in our villages. I've never cared about this conception in other tribes, but am very convinced that lots of tribes in Black Africa have, or at least had, such a conception—as I had understood it from a novel I read. The novel is *Scholarship*. The character of this book was a black congolese (Zairean) boy who went to study to Belgium. The boy considered young Belgians who used to joke with him as his own kinsmen who died years ago, and the setting of the story is the native region of the author. It is about 300 km from our tribe.
>
> Therefore, it is a belief that covers, or at least covered, more than one tribe.
>
> Still, in our villages, old people who were not at school do keep this conception despite scholars clearance.
>
> One good example is that Mrs. and Mr. Burrus are said to be grandparents of mine who died years ago. This because I have much time to deal with them. People ignore the mere reason related to one of the definitions of Language by Linguists: "Language is not only the principal medium that human beings use to communicate with each other, but also the bond that links people together and binds them to their culture."
>
> As a matter of fact, I am linked to this couple simply because I speak their language (English).
>
> This thought often comes, or came, to people when a white man makes, or made, friends with a black man, or when he gives, or gave, him lots of things.

How does a black man become white? They say (said) when during the lifetime a black man was nice (or a good christian), then after his death, he'd become a white man. And, once he found money, he'd help his kinsmen who are still living with the black skin. According to those primitive thoughts, white men are from Europe, and Europe is our churchyards.

In my point of view, this illusion is also due to the fact that when magicians go to pray to churchyards, they pretend or say they are talking with white people. This can be one of the sources that make old people uncritically believe that white men's villages are churchyards.

To end, this belief has a restricted field now, as many of those who could think so and know something about geography (for they were at school and know different continents of the world).

Yours, Francis Iyelemvela.

Bosobe July 13, 1995 (10 p.m.)

CHAPTER 10

Bosobe, Zaire

Africa, 1996

In February of 1996, George and I again made our way to Zaire and the hospital in Bosobe. We carried twenty-four boxes, seventy pounds each, full of needed medicine, insulin, and supplies for our friends of twenty-seven years. We stopped in Zurich to purchase some medical books for the young doctors that we continue to help at the University of Kinshasa Medical School, and then we left Zurich for a night in the Swiss countryside. The Wolfsprung was closed for the winter months; however, we found a small bed-and-breakfast inn in Kissnacht, Switzerland. The next morning we had an early breakfast and headed for our flight from Zurich to Kinshasa.

We flew over the Sahara Desert, landing in Liberville, Gabon, for a short stop. As the plane took off for the one-hour ride to Kinshasa, once again I reflected on many issues:

1. Why did we make the long trip again into the unknown jungle of Africa?
2. Will the boxes of medicine and relief arrive as we reach the airport in Kinshasa?
3. Will the airport be the usual zoo of disorganization and confusion?

The answer to question number one was revealed in the two weeks spent in the interior, as people responded to medicine and the opportunity to be healed by someone who cares. The answer to question number two was Yes! Once again, we were lucky to check our baggage in Nashville, Tennessee, and two days later, we picked it up in Kinshasa, Zaire, halfway around the world. The answer to question number three was a definite Yes! However, a few familiar faces met us and helped us through the confusion. It is very difficult to describe the scene within Njili Airport. We left the airport in an old car that had to be pushed off in order to catch the engine and start. We spent that night at the Methodist Presbyterian Hostel and left early the next morning for the airport and our trip up-country to Bosobe. We went through passport control, loaded up the small plane, and then a surprise and a first for our many trips. The airport authorities seized the plane, and after four hours of talking and handing over a small sum of money, we were on our way. One might say, "Such is Africa," and this would be very true. Our pilot said he must stop in Semendua to refuel, and I quickly remembered our famous stop in Semendua in 1993 when we were forced to unload and never made it to Bosobe. However, our week in Vanga was a contribution to that hospital and the people of that region.

We landed in Semendua, greeted a previous pilot and friend, Dan Carlson, and got back into the plane. The plane's engine would not turn over, and another delay was evident. Dan was an MAF pilot, and his small plane was in the hangar. He said that he would get his plane ready and take us on to Bosobe. I walked on to his house to greet his wife, Karen, and to see the children.

The Carlsons had four children and were expecting another child in late summer. It was like a flashback to 1969, and once again, I was a young mother with six children living in the interior of Africa. Karen Carlson was going to home school her children, and in memory of Ellen and Roger, we contributed some funds for the addition of a schoolroom to their small cottage. We ate lunch with the family, and then Dan, the father, took us on to Bosobe in his MAF plane.

So far it had been a long, hot day; however, the surprises were far from over for George and me. When we arrived at Bosobe, we were met with the news that our trusted cook and friend, Jacob, had been accused of stealing three mattresses from our house and would no longer be our cook. This proved to be only a small problem, since another cook was provided. However, I miss Jacob and prefer to have his services as the cook. Since he is also an old friend of twenty-seven years, we were quick to visit his home and reassure him of our trust.

I have chosen this trip as the time to finish my epic of travel, family, and life in four different cultures. However, my days and nights have been as a baby's sleep sometimes occurs. I am wide awake at night, so I write by lamp and take some naps during the day.

Once again, George was delighted to find the two young Zairean doctors working in the hospital and ready to receive our boxes of medicine and supplies. Dr. Willié and Dr. Aaron were eager to work and ready for help and instruction. They had come to Bosobe in January of 1995, and George enjoyed many hours of conversation and work with them.

I continued to oversee the kitchen, and we preferred fish as our main noon dish. As the days passed, I felt that the fish had somewhat of a different taste and texture. I finally found out that we were eating eel. Before coming back, I shall insist upon Jacob as our cook!

As part of African custom, our house is guarded day and night. During the day, two or three guards sit on the porch, discuss or argue loudly in Lingala, and greet friends passing by the house. At night, two guards ready their bows and arrows and prepare to guard. They also make up their beds and prepare to sleep. Such is African custom.

Tonight as I write by lamp, I have heard drums and singing coming from the people out in the jungle. A huge storm is brewing, and it is beginning to sound like the monsoons did in India. The rain will cool the air and make sleeping easier.

In the morning as I prepared to dress, I found a huge spider resting on my skirt. It looked like a tarantula to me. George was more intent on taking its picture than killing it.

African worship services usually last about two and one-half hours because of singing and praying. Four or five choirs sing along with drums and tambourines. Some say that music is the soul of Africans and

Our church in Bosobe.

their culture. Their music and dancing represent births, deaths, worship, war, hunting, love, and mourning.

On this trip, George brought along about one hundred baseball hats to give to the people. All hours of the day we had people knocking on our door for a hat. Soon we were passing almost everyone in the village with a bright colored hat. It reminded me of the time when we brought lots of whistles for the children and quickly realized our mistake. The Swedish missionaries rested after lunch, and every day the children paraded by their houses blowing their whistles. We finally had to give the pastor the remaining whistles because it was getting out of hand.

One day, a young man came by our house leading a small four-year-old boy. He explained that the doctor had performed a caesarean section for the baby's birth in 1991. His name was Burrus. George took his picture with a Polaroid camera, and he smiled at his image.

Another visitor on this day brought by two baby alligators about ten inches in length. He wanted to sell them to us, but no thanks!

Our trip is drawing to a close, so last night we met with the committee to discuss scholarships and the future of the hospital. It was very hard to concentrate on my French. However, it is getting somewhat easier, and George complimented my improvement.

As we prepare to leave, the people press us for a return date. I do not know why I feel so emotional each time that I leave Bosobe. The reason must be that each time I feel the sincere need of these people for our help medically to the body and friendship to the soul. As our small plane flies over this dark continent of rivers and jungles, I am again reminded of its vastness and mystery.

After landing in Kinshasa, we met with the five medical students and three nursing students to whom we are giving scholarships. During the meeting, I realized that one boy was the son of my old cook, Moise, and one was Moise's grandson. Another boy was the son of Iyuli, our gardener back in 1969. These two African friends are deceased, but twenty-seven years later, we have contact with their sons and grandson. In my wildest dreams, I would not have pictured this scenario twenty-seven years earlier.

During our last day in Kinshasa, a group of Americans from North Carolina arrived to spend two weeks up-country. They were staying at the Methodist Presbyterian Hostel where we stayed, and some conversation revealed two interesting facts. In the group was Dr. Bill Bradford from Charlotte, North Carolina. After exchanging names he replied, "As a resident at Memorial Hospital in New York in 1961, I assisted in the operation upon your father, Dr. Roger Burrus." One of the young ladies said that she worked with a Mr. Swan Burrus III in Charlotte some years ago. He now lives in Nashville and is related to our family. What a small world in some respects!

As we land in Nashville, safe once again from our trip to our friends halfway around the world, we look forward to 1996. Some plans include a family ski trip in March, the double christening of Taylor and Elizabeth in April, an internship reunion in May, a family vacation in Kiawah, South Carolina, during August, and back to Zaire in October. George and I will celebrate our forty-third wedding anniversary in June of 1996. I found the following description of love and marriage in a novel by Elizabeth Adler. This paragraph is for my daughters, grandchildren, and generations to follow.

> Love is caring for someone more than yourself, sharing your strengths and taking from his to shore up your own weaknesses. Love is understanding his life and trying to make it easier and more pleasant and he must do the same for you. It's sharing your joy in your children, seeing them through their illnesses together, and taking pride in their achievements. Love is so complex I'm not sure anyone truly understands exactly what it is—the first feelings of appeal and romance are only the foundation. Love is a long path, and to achieve it you need understanding and compassion.

As I look back on my journey of love, one thread seems to weave its way in and out of my life. That is the thread of inclusiveness.

Among my friends are citizens of Sweden, Finland, Zaire, Egypt, the U.S., South America, India, Belgium, Cayman Islands, France, Switzerland, Iran, Poland, Greece, Japan, and China.

Among my friends are members of the various Protestant denominations, Catholics, Hindus, Swedish Baptists, Jewish Faith, Baha'i Faith, and Muslims.

I have met royalty and a few famous actors and actresses, attended a gala at Blenheim Palace, visited Queen Elizabeth's private quarters at Sandringham, visited and dined with all castes of India's population from highest (Brahmin) to the lowest (the Harijans), visited Mr. Gandhi's Ashram in Porbunda, Gujarat, India, flown on President Mobutu's private plane, visited the Pygmies, had tea in the most humble African or Indian homes with dirt floors, held tiny sick African babies, and yet all of these groups share the same feelings of joy, sorrow, love, loneliness, despair, hope, and expectations of good health and family closeness.

My story is not over. I chose to finish this epic in February of 1996. However, I am keeping a journal as we go into 1996 and will continue my journey of love.

Index

Bold face numbers denote photo captions.